A TERRIBLE BEAUTY

Martin Marix Evans

Photography

David Lyons

Gill & Macmillan

Gill & Macmillan Ltd

Hume Avenue

Park West

Dublin 12

with associated companies throughout the world

www.gillmacmillan.ie

© Martin Marix Evans and David Lyons, 2003

0 7171 3542 X

Design and print origination by Fergal Norris, Outburst Design

Maps by Design Image

Colour reproduction by Ultragraphics Ltd, Dublin

Printed by Butler & Tanner Ltd, Frome

*The paper used in this book is made from the wood pulp of managed forests.
For every tree felled, at least one tree is planted, thereby renewing natural resources.*

A catalogue record is available for this book from the British Library.

1 3 5 4 2

Contents

Maps

Acknowledgments

The author is grateful to Joe Gallagher for his help in defining the coverage of this book and his encouragement in the writing of it, and to Rio Fanning who had the patience and kindness to read the draft text and give gentle guidance. The contribution of various members of the Battlefields Trust is also acknowledged. None of these is responsible for the content of the finished text.

Introduction

The inspiration for this book came from the meeting of two Irish influences: the landscape photographs of the Irishman David Lyons and the heredity of the writer. In 1860 my great-grandfather, Thomas Evans, married Elizabeth Revington in London, Ontario, Canada. Thomas was born in County Wicklow in 1836, presumably from a line of descent that originated in Wales, and Elizabeth at Roscrea, County Tipperary, in 1837. There are no family stories of famine or misery attending their emigration from Ireland or their later settlement in Buffalo, New York. Their son, John, went to England in 1903 and ten years later married a Frenchwoman. Their eldest son married a girl from Cumberland. She was of northern English and Scottish descent, producing a cocktail of national loyalties that makes it impossible to be partisan in considering the history of Europe.

David Lyons's people, both on his father's and his mother's side, have farmed the land of the ancient kingdom of Dál Riada on Ireland's northern coast for many generations. Since prehistoric times it has been a place apart, looking as much to the Hebridean Islands and Scottish coastline as to the south. The people of this place, whom the Picts across the water called skirmishers, Scotii, established a sister kingdom in Argyll and Kintyre, nurturing Columba's Irish Christian church on Iona and gradually dominating the country that now bears their name.

In the light of this background, political borders are not considered a thing of permanence. What is more significant is the way in which the Irish landscape divides naturally by means of rivers and mountains, bays and bogs. These place limitations on movement and sight, limitations that shape battles and constrain armies; and these are the influences that have led to the dividing of this book into its six distinct chapters.

The great beauty of the Irish countryside, so well captured by David Lyons, conceals former scenes of both brutality and heroism. It was to investigate what happened in these places that this book was written. The land itself has had a profound influence on military events and often one particular place, the Moyry Pass, for example, is the site of battle after battle down through the centuries. This is why the photographs are so important. The Moyry Pass, deceptively mild and lovely, is a very defensible pass against an enemy and a daunting challenge to an attacker. Why try to convey in words what can so much better be shown in pictures? And words themselves deserve their place without intervention from me, which is why quotations, with all the flavour and spelling of their time, are offered in the place of paraphrase.

Measured against the sweep of time, today's conflicts and convictions appear puny and transient. What emerges clearly from the hunt for battlegrounds is that the island nature of Ireland has been of limited relevance to events taking place within its shoreline. People have been coming and going from Ireland since ancient times and events on the island have always been intimately connected with what was taking place elsewhere. The flow of trade and raid between Ireland and lands to the north, east and south, and latterly to the west, should have created links far wider than this one island can contain. Better by far to look at the land, work out the story of what happened in and on that land, and then seek to understand. Given the choice between Yeats and Southey, I'm with Southey.

All changed, changed utterly;
A terrible beauty is born.
Easter 1916, W.B. Yeats

But what they fought each other for,
I could not well make out …
And everybody praised the Duke,
Who this great fight did win.
But what good came of it at last?
Quoth little Peterkin.
Why, that I cannot tell, said he,
But 'twas a famous victory.
The Battle of Blenheim, *Robert Southey*

Martin Marix Evans,
Blakesley 2003

1

Dublin and the Pale

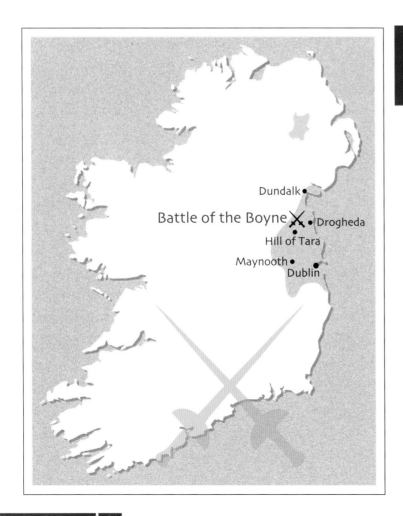

Dundalk•
Battle of the Boyne ✕ •Drogheda
•
Hill of Tara
Maynooth• •
Dublin

In times of peace and stability no land is more valuable than rich pasture and fertile planting ground, but when the blast of war blows through the land such pleasant places become hard to defend. Perhaps it was for this reason that the area eventually to become known as the Pale was first settled inland, safe from sea-borne marauders. In the search for the fields that now give soft cover to the sites of great battles, the most ancient marker is the symbolically significant Hill of Tara.

Tara pre-dates the historical record and there is little an explorer of military happenings can say of the neolithic passage

Although best known for its symbolic standing as the seat of the High Kings, Tara is not without military advantages in the midst of the low country above the plain of the Boyne.

A representation of, it appears, a Viking ship with animal head prow and stern from Dunluce Castle, County Antrim.

tomb or, indeed, in terms of verifiable events, of the hillfort itself. What is clear is the iconic importance of the place on the ridge between Navan and Dunshaughlin as the seat of the High Kings of Ireland. There it occupies the centre of a semi-circle overlooking the sea and bounded in the north by the mountains, beyond which lies Ulster, in the west by the bog and the complex waterways of the Shannon, and in the south by the mountains of Wicklow. The southern half of the semi-circle lies in Leinster where the Uí Dúnlainge held sway in the ninth century; the northern part is in Meath, the territory of the Southern Uí Néill. The grip of the latter on the High Kingship was loosened not by a Leinsterman, however, but by the ruler of Munster, Brian Bórumha, frequently called Brian Boru.

The Battle of Clontarf

As the first millennium approached, the control of Ireland was fragmented among a number of Irish leaders and kings, but with a significant admixture of Viking influence. The Ostmen, mainly from Norway, had started raids on Ireland within a year or so of those on Scotland and England, in A.D.795, and in the next thirty years their attacks spread to include the far south-west of the country. Raiding gave way to settlement, temporary to begin with – mere over-wintering camps such as in

Dublin in 841 to 842 – and attacks were launched from there, but now the Ostmen began to ally themselves with Irish rulers as well. As time passed they became part of the warring, fragmented and bloody tapestry of the land's power structure and also, from their coastal settlements, the builders of Ireland's first towns and the creators of substantial international trade.

The southern Shannon basin, the northern limit of Munster, formed the kingdom of Thomond. Here, in the middle of the tenth century, the Dál Cais rose to power as the traditional rulers of Munster declined in strength. Brian Boru succeeded to the kingship after his brother, Mathghamhain, was assassinated in 976. He took vengeance on the killers, the Ostmen of Limerick among them, at the battle of Inis Cathaig in 977 and then proceeded to extend his influence. He formed an alliance with the Ostmen of Waterford in order to gain sea-power with which to challenge the Uí Néill. The High King, Máel Sechnaill II of the southern Uí Néill, met him at Clonfert in 997 and agreed to divide Ireland with him, giving Brian Boru dominion over Leinster and Dublin. When the rulers of Leinster and Dublin rose against him in 999, Brian defeated them at the Battle of Glen Máma, west of Dublin, and then besieged the town. He sacked Dublin and reduced its king, Sitric Silkenbeard, not merely to submission but to taking an active part in Brian's quest for greater power. In 1002 Máel Sechnaill was forced to concede the High Kingship of Tara to Brian Boru. By 1011 Brian Boru was closer to being a *de facto* High King in actual control of Ireland than any man before him and had demonstrated that the position could be much more than a fine title.

Sitric did not remain submissive for long. With Máel Mórda, King of Leinster, he rose against Brian. Help was sought from Brodar of the Isle of Man and from Orkney, where Sigurd II ruled. Sigurd had acquired considerable power with the acquisition of Caithness, Sutherland and Ross from Malcolm II, whom he had recognised as ruler of the Scottish mainland and whose daughter, Donada, he married, thus becoming step-father to Macbeth. In return for his support Sigurd was offered the High Kingship by Sitric, a clear threat of a Viking takeover, though whether Máel Mórda knew of this is not clear. Sitric offered further inducements, promising his mother's hand in marriage to Sigurd. *Njal's Saga*, the Icelandic story of Njal Thorgeisson, says that the lady Kormlada (Gormlaith in Irish) 'was the fairest of all women' but does not specify her age; presumably she was a credible bribe. What Donada thought of this is not known to us, and perhaps the idea was unknown to her as well. The confusion is increased by the report that Sitric made the same offer to Brodar.

Brodar prepared twenty ships and his brother Ospak had ten which he was invited to bring to Dublin on Palm Sunday, as the other Ostmen had agreed to do. Ospak declined, being unwilling to fight so good a king as Brian Boru, and the brothers parted in anger. That night Brodar and his host were awakened by a great noise and sprang up to discover they were being showered with boiling blood, and many were scalded. The next night they awoke to find their weapons engaged in combat with each other and the third night they were attacked by ravens and were obliged to fight them off with their swords. Each night these torments took the life of one man from each ship. Somewhat concerned, Brodar went to Ospak to seek an interpretation of these omens. Ospak, cautious of his brother's possible reaction, obtained an assurance that there was peace between them, but made the assurance doubly sure by delaying his response until after nightfall, as Brodar 'never slew a man by night'.

The explanation was as follows: The boiling blood foretold much bloodshed, of others and their own. The great noise was the crack of doom, a portent of swift death. The fighting weapons indicated a battle and the ravens were the devils that would drag them off to hell. Brodar was not pleased, but as it was night he retired to plan the slaughter of his brother and his brother's men on the morrow. Ospak slipped away before dawn and placed his forces in the service of Brian Boru. The details are difficult to vouch for, but the tale does offer an explanation of a known fact, that Ostmen fought on both sides at Clontarf. Some may have come from Limerick, in Brian Boru's personal fief, but others may well have been men of Man.

As Easter drew near the forces gathered around Dublin. Within the town Máel Mórda's Leinstermen and Sitric's Ostmen were ready and in the countryside Brian's forces – Dál gCais, Munstermen and men of Galway, with a leavening of Ostmen, all under the command of Brian Boru's son Murchadh – plundered what they could. When this had gone on long enough to thoroughly irritate the forces in Dublin they decided to come out and give battle. It was Good Friday, 23 April 1014. The Leinster-Ostmen army, having crossed the Liffey, marched north-east, crossed the little River Tolka and faced their adversaries in the area of Clontarf. An Irish description of the battle, *The War of the Gaedhil with the Gaill*, gives a few clues to the nature of the terrain and the weather that day. Máel Sechnaill was present, but for reasons never explained did not fight for Brian Boru with whom he was allegedly allied. He did, however, report:

> There was a field, and a ditch, between us [Brian's army] and them, and the sharp wind of spring coming over the field towards us …

Elsewhere there is a reference to limitations on the flanks of the field of battle. A wood was on one side and 'the head of Dubhghall's Bridge' on the other, with sea to the rear of the Dublin men, but for all this the scene remains unclear, a fact which, after the passage of a thousand years, is not surprising. Exactly where it is in relation to the modern landscape is equally hard to decide, as most of the area has been built on.

Neither the same source nor *Njal's Saga* enable us to guess the formations with a significant degree of accuracy, for the two accounts are fundamentally different. According to the Saga Brian's army had his grandson, Turlough (Toirdhealbhach), commanding the centre with Ospak on one side and Wolf the Quarrelsome on the other. Facing Wolf was Brodar of Man and Sitric stood opposite Ospak, while Sigurd commanded the centre and the Leinstermen go unremarked. The Irish account has the opposing formations in three lines, with Brian Boru's army having

Near the point at which the River Tolka enters Dublin Bay, housing conceals the site of the Battle of Clontarf.

his Dál gCais contingent in the front, the Munstermen in the second line and the Connacht warriors in the third line; no mention of Ostmen. On the other side the Ostmen were in front with the Dublin force in the second line and the Leinster forces forming the third line. What appears to be undisputed is that the fighting revolved around a few prominent heroes and that it was amazingly ferocious.

The weapons and protective clothing worn by the men as described in these accounts is probably misrepresented by the work of subsequent scribes or story-tellers. Given the period, not long before the well-documented and illustrated fights of 1066 in England, the Vikings were certainly wearing mail byrnies, garments popularly called chain-mail shirts, and conical helmets, perhaps with a nasal or nose-guard. No one ever wore the horned helmet beloved of Hollywood movies; one blow of an axe to a projecting horn would have twisted the head and broken the wearer's neck as swiftly as a hangman's rope. The weapons were principally the axe and the straight-bladed sword, with some spears and bows also used. The Irish equipment would have been similar except that mail shirts were rare and leather jackets more common. They also made more use of spears as throwing, and often as stabbing, weapons.

They faced one another across that field and ditch, with the cold, thin wind blowing from the west and the sun starting to climb the sky. If the accounts are true, the survivors would still be there to see it set as the battle ended.

As Good Friday was a fast day, a day of religious observance, Brian would not fight. That he was over seventy years of age might also have been a factor. The saga says that a shieldburg, a wall of warriors' shields, was thrown round him while the Irish account seems to position him some distance from the conflict, in the company of a single attendant who observed the fight while his king prayed, sang psalms and recited paternosters. The battle began, in one version, with single combat between the son of the King of Lochlann, Plait, and an Irish champion, Domhnall, son of the high steward of Alba. The Viking went looking for his adversary, shouting, 'Where is Domhnall?' until the reply came, 'Here, thou reptile!' They fell upon each other and fought to the death, collapsing each with the other's sword through his heart and the hair of his head grasped in his free hand.

Brodar slaughtered many men of Wolf the Quarrelsome until he came face to face with Wolf himself. Twice Brodar was thrown to the ground by the force of Wolf's blows but he was not wounded and was able to take shelter in the wood. On the other flank Ospak cut his way through his enemies and put Sitric Silkenbeard to flight. In the centre Turlough and his men struck at Sigurd's Orkneymen, laying low the Dublin king's front line and breaking through to kill his banner-bearer. Sigurd ordered one Thorstein Hallson to take it up, but another man shouted that all who did so would die. Sigurd himself gathered up the banner, tore it from its staff and thrust it under his cloak.

The account given in *The War of the Gaedhil with the Gaill* speaks of Sigurd's fate. As the day drew on and many of the Ostmen fled, Murchadh, son of Brian Boru, saw Sigurd doing terrible damage to Turlough's Dál gCais,

> slaughtering and mutilating them; and his fury among them was as of a robber upon a plain; and neither pointed nor any other kind of edged weapon could harm him.

Murchadh, fighting with a sword in each hand, rushed upon Sigurd and struck with his right hand, slicing through the fastenings of Sigurd's helmet, knocking it from his head. Then Murchadh brought the sword in his left hand round to cut deep into Sigurd's neck. Thus the 'brave hero', as *The War* calls the enemy, died. The Dál gCais were next beset by Ebric, son of the King of Lochlann, hacking his way through them and again Murchadh went to their aid. He turned on the 'mailed-men' and slew fifteen on each hand as he hewed his way towards his chosen adversary, melting the very inlay of his sword-blade with the ferocity of his attack. The heat was so great that he was forced to throw his sword aside and, grabbing Ebric's mail hood, heaved his coat over his head and wrestled him to the ground. Murchadh seized the foreigner's sword and drove it through his chest and into the earth beneath him, pulled it out, thrust it back and then pinned him down a third time. Ebric, meanwhile, drew a knife,

> and with it gave Murchadh such a cut, that the whole of his entrails were cut out, and they fell to the ground before him. Then did shiverings and faintings

descend on Murchadh, and he had not the power to move, so that they fell by each other there, the foreigner and Murchadh. But at the same time Murchadh cut off the foreigner's head. And Murchadh did not die that night, nor until sunrise the next day.

The battle lasted, the Irish chronicler says, from one high tide to the next and, in a passage rather hard to understand, he suggests that the tide carried away their ships so that they could not flee. As they fell back they were caught between the wood and Dubhghall's Bridge and had nowhere to go but into the sea itself. Not all of them ran; the saga says Turlough came upon Thorstein Hallson doing up his shoelace and asked him why he was not running away. 'Because,' said Thorstein, 'I can't get home tonight, since I am at home in Iceland.' Turlough let him go, but, according to the Irish account, gave chase to others right into the sea. There, while grasping an enemy in each hand, a wave threw him against the weir of Clontarf and one of the stakes went clean through him, killing him.

As dusk drew near the field was Brian Boru's, but the king remained at his prayers. His attendant gave him news of the battle's progress and the fall of his son's standard. The battle was won but not all of the enemy had been put to flight, for Brodar emerged from his hiding place and came at Brian Boru with a battle-axe. Brian defended himself with his sword, but the invader cut him down. The Irish version has it that Brian Boru cut Brodar's left leg off at the knee and his right at the foot before Brodar clove his head in two and the two fell dead side by side. But the saga has an even more colourful version of events.

According to the saga, Brodar saw that Brian Boru's men were in hot pursuit of the Vikings and Leinstermen, leaving the shieldburg under-manned. He immediately broke through and attacked the king. The attendant, Takt, threw his arm in front of his master but both it and his master's head were severed. Brian's blood fell on Takt's arm-stump and it healed instantly, but the king was dead and Brodar bellowed his triumph. Wolf the Quarrelsome and Turlough, who in this version is still alive at this stage of the conflict, turned back, surrounded the men of Man and subdued them by throwing tree branches on them. Wolf then took Brodar and cut his belly, pulled out his entrails and wound them out of him by making him walk round and round a tree. 'He did not die,' the saga asserts, 'before they were all drawn out of him.'

The Leinster-Dublin Ostmen alliance had been defeated but Brian Boru's tenure of the High Kingship expired with him, leaving Máel Sechnaill to resume the position. He could not, however, aspire to the same dominance and the High King of Tara never again wielded the power that Brian Boru had commanded, the country continuing in division into lesser kingdoms. Indeed, after Máel Sechnaill's death in 1022 the title went unclaimed for half a century. The Vikings exploited the victory and their occupation of the coastal cities continued, bringing trade and wealth to the land. Sitric Silkenbeard continued to rule in Dublin until 1035 and, while the kings of Leinster had control from 1046 with one brief interval, Ostmen ruled the city until 1170.

The Arrival of the Normans

The Irish kings of the eleventh and twelfth centuries grew mighty within their own kingdoms and continued to vie with one another for supremacy. The King of Connacht, Ruaidhri Ó Conchobhair, or in the anglicised form, Rory O'Connor, was confident enough in 1166 to levy a tax of 4,000 cows on Ireland in order to pay for the loyalty of the Ostmen of Dublin. Not only did this demonstrate a degree of centralised power in the region under his control, it also underlined the crucial importance of Dublin to anyone who entertained ambitions to rule Ireland as a whole, High King or not. The rival to this dominance was the king of the Uí Néill, Muircheartach Mac Lochlainn, who enjoyed the support of the king of Leinster, Diarmaid MacMurchadha (Dermot MacMurrough), and with the death of the former that same year the latter was forced out of the land by the allies of the king of Connacht, the new High King.

Throughout Europe, Norman influence was spreading while at the same time shared religious belief and the pursuit of scholarship drew people together in something approaching a community of civilised interests. Ireland was no exception to this trend, apart from, until now, its Norman contingent. In England these conquerors had been in power for a century and thought of themselves as English, the scholars tell us. What the Anglo-Saxons and Welsh thought they were receives less attention; even in twenty-first century Northamptonshire men can be found who will curse the Duke of Grafton, responsible for the deforestation and enclosure of the Whittlewood Forest in 1824, as the man who plucked away rights patiently regained from the previous set of thieves, the Normans, who declared it a Royal Forest in the first place. The intervention of Pope Adrian IV, an Englishman (though probably a Norman), was contrived by Theobald, Archbishop of Canterbury, who opposed the reduction of his influence over Irish church affairs. As a result, in 1155, a letter know as *Laudabiliter* was sent by the pontiff to grant Henry II of England the right to invade Ireland and reform the Irish church. He did nothing of the kind, either then or later, for he was much too interested in the control and exploitation of an empire that stretched as far south as the Pyrenees. His son, Richard I, would spend only six months in all his ten-year reign in England, which is some measure of the country's standing in comparison with more southerly lands. What did happen, eleven years on from Adrian's letter, was the arrival of the ousted king of Leinster at the court of the English king.

Diarmaid went to England to seek help in regaining his kingdom and to this end approached Henry. The king of England was not interested, though he was not opposed to the idea, and was happy enough to accept fealty from the Irishman and to give permission for Diarmaid to recruit assistance from within his domains. The feudal system was well established by this time, and the law of primogeniture – the passing of lands and titles to the first-born son – left a number of spare knights, second and third sons, around. Not only were these men eager for expeditions and gain, they were also sped on their way by kinsmen only too pleased to bid them farewell. Diarmaid found the men he needed in Wales and in August 1167 he returned, eventually succeeding in reclaiming his kingdom. Two sons of Nesta

Ferch Rhys, a Welsh princess who married Gerald de Windsor, castellan of Carew Castle in Pembroke, and who was famed for her beauty and numerous lovers, joined Diarmaid, Maurice FitzGerald and Robert FitzStephen in May 1169. The chronicler Gerald of Wales (Geraldus Cambrensis) was the grandson of the lovely Nesta and thus inclined to give prominence to his two uncles. Raymond le Gros arrived a year later. Exactly when his greatest ally, Richard Fitz Gilbert de Clare, agreed to join him is less clear, probably after FitzGerald and FitzStephen had helped Diarmaid secure southern Leinster, but he arrived in August 1170.

Diarmaid's promise to de Clare, who was to become known as Strongbow, was that he should have the hand of his daughter, Aoife (Eva), and would inherit Leinster in due time. Strongbow brought two hundred knights and about a thousand others to Waterford and the town was taken before they moved on the essential conquest, Dublin. Their approach was no surprise and the ruler of the city, Astell (Haskulf) Ragnaldson, made ready to defend the place. Ruaidhri Ó Conchobhair (Rory O'Connor) of Connacht came to his aid together with men of the kingdoms to his

The effigy marking what is traditionally known as Strongbow's tomb in Christ Church Cathedral, Dublin, is an excellent representation of a knight of that period. Under the surcoat the figure is clad in mail and it carries a Norman kite-shaped shield.

east, Breifne and Meath (Midhe). Strongbow's route was not foreseen. It seems he came by the valley of Glendalough and what was later to be the line of the Military Road through the mountains of Wicklow to appear under the walls of Dublin in September 1170. The archbishop of Dublin, Laurence, encouraged negotiation and while discussions were in progress Raymond le Gros and Miles de Cogan burst into the city and over-ran it, slaughtering a considerable number of the inhabitants. Astell and many others took flight by sea. Then followed a general invasion of Meath, but it led to little, for Diarmaid died in May 1171.

Ruaidhri Ó Conchobhair was not content to let matters rest. Soon after the death of the king of Leinster, and the presumed succession of Strongbow, Astell Ragnaldson was back, supported by Ostmen from Scotland and the Isle of Man, to join Ruaidhri in an attack on Dublin. Astell arrived first and could not bring himself to wait for his Irish ally. The city was, at that time, very small and stood around the mound that later became Dublin Castle. As was their wont, the Normans made a sortie to oppose their attackers and met them somewhere near the present Dame Street. Miles de Cogan's men were getting the worst of it when he sent his brother Richard on a foray swinging round by the south and east to take Astell Ragnaldson in the rear and compromise his lines to his ships. Caught between the two forces the Ostmen were crushed and Astell was captured and executed.

Ruaidhri Ó Conchobhair persisted. His Connacht force encamped at Castleknock, to the west and north of the Liffey, together with the allies of the previous encounter while the men of Ulaidh, now Antrim and Down, were at Clontarf, north-east, and yet more men, Leinstermen who were unwilling to accept Strongbow as king, were at Dalkey, to the south-east on the coast. The Normans were not only seriously outnumbered, but also unsupported, for Henry II, angry at Strongbow's rise to power while on an unauthorised frolic of his own, had declared a blockade of supplies, so there was to be no help from England. By September Strongbow had been forced to open negotiations with Ruaidhri Ó Conchobhair, but all he was offered was lordship of the cities of Dublin, Wexford and Waterford, Leinster being forfeit. Caught between a rock and a hard place, the reaction was typically robust. As Maurice FitzGerald observed, they were Englishmen in the eyes of the Irish and Irish in the eyes of the English and thus obliged to depend on themselves alone. They resolved to attack.

The Norman knight was the most daunting fighting machine in Europe at this time. He wore a mail coat and mail hose (leggings). The conical helmets of William the Conqueror's time, fashioned out of four riveted segments, were being replaced by one-piece, flat-topped, cylindrical headgear with fixed face-guards. The kite-shaped shield was shorter and easier to use both on foot and mounted. The knight's horse was still relatively light, compared to the massive, cart-horse style of mount needed in the Middle Ages, but a great deal heavier than the ponies of their adversaries who, in any case, almost always fought on foot. Finally, the charge with the couched lance, a long spear held in one hand with the shaft tucked under the arm, was becoming the usual tactic in attack. The method had been used successfully by Robert Guiscard and by his son Bohemond in Italy and on crusade at the end of the previous century. Such

The Record Tower, Dublin Castle.

Dame Street, site of the Norman sortie from the castle mound. City Hall stands to the right and Trinity College is in the distance.

A later Norman knight with a helmet fitted with cheek-guards, plate armour and a smaller, though still kite-shaped, shield, from Jerpoint Abbey, County Kilkenny.

a charge was vulnerable to well-trained archers who might take out the horses. In addition to the knights, the Normans had developed the use of archers substantially since their victory at Hastings, making particular use of the skills of the Welsh. The Irish used neither armoured cavalry nor archers, but relied on swords, spears and battle-axes, and personal armour was rare. It must have been with some confidence in their success that Strongbow and his men prepared themselves for action.

Strongbow and Maurice FitzGerald led the centre column with Raymond le Gros and Miles de Cogan to the right and left. The centre included some Leinstermen and Dubliners, but for the most part this was a Norman fighting array. In the early afternoon they went swiftly out of the town to the west along the south bank of the Liffey before turning north over the bridge and riding on to the valley of the River Tolka. There they wheeled to the west once more, riding north of the area now occupied by the Phoenix Park, and fell on the unsuspecting Irish at Castleknock. Ruaidhri Ó Conchobhair, it is said, was in his bath, but managed to escape. Many were less fortunate. With the rout of the main force the other groups dispersed, leaving Strongbow master of the field.

Over-mighty lords did not appeal to kings such as Henry II and he took immediate steps to rein in his renegade vassal. While Strongbow was dealing with various citizens of Leinster who opposed his regime, Henry gathered a disciplinary expedition in England. Wisely the new king of Leinster hurried to make his peace, meeting Henry at Newnham, on the banks of the River Severn in Gloucestershire. After some spirited discussion Strongbow yielded Dublin and its environs to Henry as well as the other coastal towns and, in return, his fief of Leinster was recognised and he renewed his vows of fealty. He did not, however, retain Meath which he had taken in company with his late father-in-law. That was awarded to Henry's man, Hugh de Lacy, who also had Dublin in his care.

Henry II came to Waterford where the deal with Strongbow was confirmed and where the men of Wexford delivered up Robert FitzStephen whom they had captured. Like Strongbow, FitzStephen had been acting without the king's approval, but he was forgiven, though not rewarded with land or title. Diarmaid MacCarthaigh (Dermot MacCarthy) king of Cork, swore fealty as did Domhnall Mór O'Brien, king of Limerick, and half a dozen others. This meant that they avoided having to accept Strongbow as an overlord and, indeed, could appeal directly to Henry should the Norman incomers create difficulties. A synod was arranged to be held at Cashel during the following winter to deal with the alleged irregularities in church affairs and the results caused the new Pope, Alexander III, to confirm the standing Adrian had granted the Plantagenet king. The outcome was the division of Ireland into the English 'Lordship of Ireland', Leinster and Munster, broadly speaking, and the Irish part of the country under the Treaty of Windsor struck in 1175 with Ruaidhri Ó Conchobhair. It was an inherently unstable arrangement but it was to last for some four centuries during which the new settlers and the old quarrelled on a subdued scale that permitted a tolerable co-existence.

What had changed significantly was the position of Ireland within Europe. Whereas

The Cathedral, Cormac's Chapel and the Round Tower on the Rock of Cashel, County Tipperary.

the balance of events had been strongly directed towards Irish affairs with the odd external interruption, such as a Viking raid, the impact of power struggles far away was now felt here. Indeed, quarrels fomented abroad sometimes came to a head with blows in Ireland for no Irish reason at all, but caused lasting damage to the people of the island. Conversely, Irish-born men became involved in external disputes. This would continue for centuries to come. In 1296 twenty-eight lords in Ireland were summoned by Edward I to present themselves at Whitehaven in Cumberland on 1 March with specific numbers of men and horse for a specific period of service against Scotland. The total came to 3,157 men who embarked on more than 150 ships from Dublin, Drogheda and Carrickfergus. The force included 27 crossbowmen and 261 hobelars – a uniquely Irish contribution. A hobelar was a mounted spearman as opposed to a lance-carrying knight. He rode a small, nimble horse and could work in rough, close country such as the terrain of the Southern Uplands of Scotland. Indeed, the success of these troops was such that Edward introduced similar light cavalry into his English service.

With the distraction of the Wars of the Roses the impact of English affairs on events in Ireland declined and the great families of Butler in Ormond and FitzGerald in Desmond and Kildare represented the English interest together with the families of the Pale, the seriously English-orientated hinterland running from Dublin to Drogheda and Dundalk. Loyalties and control in England were even more uncertain and evanescent. This was to change after the victory of Henry Tudor over Richard III at Bosworth in 1485.

The Tudor Grip

Changes were slow in coming and while his rule was new, Henry VII was careful not to try too hard. Even the error of the FitzGeralds in supporting Lambert Simnel's and Perkin Warbeck's risings against Henry VII brought no more than Sir Edward Poyning's summoning of a parliament in Drogheda in 1494 to declare the English legislature supreme. The unrest that followed the eighth Earl of Kildare's imprisonment led to his reinstatement as Lord Deputy in 1496, a position he held until his death in 1513. The English king could not, at this time, do without Kildare.

In 1534 Henry VIII broke ties with the Catholic Church through the Act of Supremacy and English attention was focused on the Reformation and its consequences. The Kildares chose just this moment to bring long-running disputes to a head. Gerald FitzGerald, Gearóid Óg, the ninth Earl, had been in and out of power as Lord Deputy and his last tenure began in 1532. In August 1533 he began moving guns out of Dublin Castle in case he needed them for his own purposes. Early the next year he was summoned to London and, unable to excuse himself, he went, leaving his son Lord Offaly, known as Silken Thomas (Tomás an tSíoda), in charge. On 11 June 1534 Silken Thomas staged a theatrical resignation, accompanied by outspoken criticism of English policy, before the Privy Council in Dublin. It was a miscalculation in response to a message from his father; all that was intended was a restoration of Kildare power. In the tense atmosphere of

A hobelar, mounted on a light horse and riding without stirrups. He wears a conical helmet and a mail coat and wields a spear. From a mural in the Carmelite Priory, Clare Island, County Mayo.

religious upheaval the reaction of Henry VIII was vigorous. Sir William Skeffington, one of the few Englishmen able enough, or even willing, to work in Ireland, was appointed Deputy once again. On 27 July the fleeing archbishop, John Alen, was captured when his ship ran aground at Clontarf and was 'hacked … in gobbets' by Lord Offaly's men. Silken Thomas proceeded to besiege Dublin Castle, declare a Catholic crusade, imprison men of the Pale, and, most dangerous of all, seek help from Rome and from the Emperor Charles V before Skeffington arrived in October. By then his father, Gearóid Óg, who had been imprisoned in the Tower of London on 29 June after his son had cut loose, had died. In London it was said that all of English origin – man, woman and child – were being killed.

The Skeffington expeditionary force was, in fact, a sadly cobbled-together affair. At first it had consisted of a mere 150 men. Then it was augmented to a theoretical 1,500. Eventually 900 men sailed from Bristol and 1,600 from Chester, three months after the appointment of Skeffington to lead them. They were not helped by the lack of weapons, for longbows from Ludlow Castle were found to be defective, handguns were in short supply and the delays had led to serious losses among the horses. It sounds like a fairly typical British overseas military foray. What they did have was most impressive ordnance for the time; the weapons included two demi-cannon and two demi-culverins.

Silken Thomas, now Earl of Kildare, realised his siege of Dublin Castle could not succeed because of the feebleness of his guns. As Skeffington's force approached, Silken Thomas opened fire on the fleet. He checked, but failed to halt, the relief force and by late October had withdrawn to his castle at Maynooth, west of the city. It was not until spring that Skeffington, who at seventy years of age was too old for battle, moved against him. Support for Silken Thomas had dwindled and he was left with a force of a few hundred horse, kern (Irish footsoldiers) and gallowglass (mercenaries). The outer defences of Maynooth Castle fell after an artillery bombardment followed by an assault, but the main castle held on until, in return for a bribe, the constable, Christopher Paris, yielded on 23 March 1535. He and twenty-five others were then executed, in spite of the fact that they had not forced the attackers to storm the castle. The event was dubbed 'The Pardon of Maynooth' and became a by-word for a betrayal of trust.

Silken Thomas fought on, making a series of raids which the English found hard to handle, until he was persuaded to surrender to Lord Leonard Grey, his uncle, on 25 August. The undertaking to spare his life turned out to be as unreliable as that given to his constable and, together with five of his uncles, he died at Tyburn in London on 3 February 1537. Grey became Lord Deputy and embarked on a campaign of castle destruction and oppression that caused him to be called the Earl of Kildare newly-born again. He himself was removed from office in 1540 and executed for treason a year later.

The Kildare rebellion spelt the end of the old arrangements for the governance of Ireland and brought the expensive alternative of direct rule. The conduct of the campaign on both sides gave an indication of the levels of savagery which would accompany future disputes.

The Cromwellian Campaign

The difficulty facing Ireland when the English were having their Civil War was deciding which side to support. In 1641 a Catholic rising by Old English in the Pale and the Ulster Irish started a war in which James Butler, fourth Earl of Ormond, and Robert Munroe in command of Scottish troops, sought to suppress the rebels. The major suffering occurred in Ulster and there were mass killings – much exaggerated in the reports that reached England. But then the English Parliament and the English king found themselves at war and the former was allied with the Scots, so Munroe and the Earl of Ormond were now adversaries! The Catholics established themselves as a confederation based in Kilkenny with whom Charles I reached an understanding, so Ormond was able to send troops to the king while Munroe, for the Scots and thus for Parliament, was left to endure as best he could in Antrim, north-east Ulster.

The Earl of Ormond did not manage to wring much more out of the Catholic Confederation, though in 1644 2,000 troops were sent to Scotland to serve under the marquis of Montrose, with outstanding success. The Scots were also hard pressed in Ulster, where they were comprehensively beaten at Benburb. The

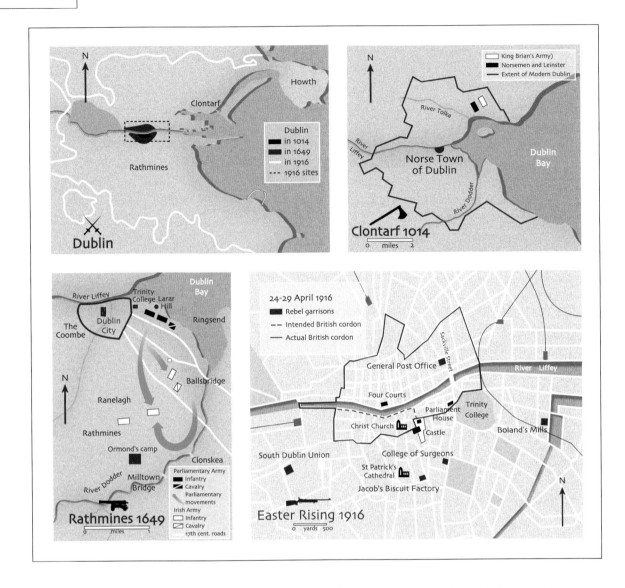

Confederation fractured when some stood firm in support of Charles I and others were determined to gain freedom for Catholics, taking the argument as far as excommunicating those who did not co-operate. The Earl of Ormond, still hoping that king and Parliament in England would forge a peace, handed Dublin over to a Parliamentarian force under Colonel Michael Jones on 18 June 1647, together with Drogheda, Dundalk, Naas and Trim. He had unwittingly contrived exactly what the Confederation most wished to avoid: allowing the Puritan Parliament a foothold in Ireland.

The Leinster Confederates reacted at once and Thomas Preston brought his army to besiege Trim. The Confederate forces comprised 1,000 horse, 7,000 foot and four 12-pounder demi-culverins. Preston was an expert in the art of siege warfare, but, as events were to prove, less effective in the field. Michael Jones brought 800 horse, 4,000 foot and seven guns from Dublin and also had at his command 700 horse, 1,200 foot and two more guns coming from Drogheda to meet him at Skreen, east of Trim. Preston moved, but not as expected, making instead for Portlester. To

Trim Castle, County Meath. Trim was more an administrative centre than a military base and its fortifications, while impressive, were intended to enforce subservience without having to fight for it.

tempt him away Jones attacked Tremblestown Castle, which was held by Confederates. The Confederates then made a relaxed march for Dublin, but Michael Jones used his cavalry and the energetic progress of his army to bring the battle to him at Dungan's Hill, near Lynch's Knock, now Summerhill.

The position was not well chosen. Among its shortcomings was the standing wheat on the ridge which obscured their sight lines and a bog below which limited their ability to manoeuvre. Jones attacked the Irish right and his men were charged three times by Preston's 'redshanks', the Antrim and West Highland Catholic Scots under Alasdair MacDonald. The kilted warriors, in spite of their determination, were eventually overcome and Jones's cavalry drove off the Confederate horse so the remaining infantry were forced to fall back into the bog where they were destroyed. Only about 500 of them escaped, leaving more than 2,000 dead and wounded behind them. The Parliamentarian foothold in Ireland was secure.

The outbreak of the Second Civil War in England changed the situation once again. Charles reached agreement with the Scots and they invaded England, only to be

Dungan's Hill, now presenting the peaceful image of a country estate rather than the killing fields of 8 August 1647. The house, Summerfield, was the birthplace of the Duke of Wellington.

In the ghostly light of the crypt of Christ Church Cathedral, the battered statues of Charles I and Charles II stand disgraced, removed from their positions on City Hall.

beaten by Oliver Cromwell's forces in Lancashire in July and August 1648. The Earl of Ormond returned from exile in France to Ireland in September and put together a merged Confederate and royalist force which, after the execution of the king of England and of Scotland on 30 January 1649 on the verdict of the English Parliament, transferred its loyalties to his son. The alliance included Murrough O'Brien, Earl of Inchiquin, the victor of the battle of Knockanauss in Cork the previous November, who had defected from the Parliamentarian cause in April, but the adherence of Owen Roe O'Neill was lacking. O'Neill had been a stalwart of the Catholic Confederation, but sided with the papal nuncio, Giovanni Battista Rinuccini, who had been so ready to excommunicate potential allies to his cause.

In June 1649 the Earl of Ormond moved on the Pale with a force of some 11,000 men. The Earl of Inchiquin took Drogheda, Dundalk, Newry and Trim before joining Ormond at Finglas, north of Dublin, with 4,000 men to add to the 1,500 horse and 5,000 foot already there. Having come to the conclusion that an assault across the Liffey was not likely to succeed, they left 2,500 men there and took the rest to Rathmines, due south of the city and overlooking it. The city walls were close to the Liffey, north of the present line of the Grand Canal and even Trinity College stood outside them. Baggotrath Castle stood near the present Baggot Street Bridge over the canal. Ranelagh, Rathmines, Donnybrook and Ballsbridge were all very much open country, which Ormond apparently admired without doing anything of importance other than blockading the city by land. In the meantime Oliver Cromwell had been appointed Lord Lieutenant of Ireland by the English Parliament and had a force of 8,000 foot, 3,000 horse and 1,200 dragoons ready to depart for Ireland. Michael Jones spread the rumour that Cromwell was bound for Munster and the Earl of Inchiquin was detached to organise the defence of the area, taking three regiments of horse with him. On 26 July the first of the Parliamentarian force arrived in Dublin from Chester, making a nonsense of the blockade and bringing Jones's force to numbers almost the equal of Ormond's.

Uncertainty hamstrung Ormond's counsels. Some of his advisers were in favour of withdrawing while others suggested taking out the enemy force at Rathfarnham Castle, close by. On 28 July they did just that, and were so cheered by their success that an attack to secure the rich pastures of Donnybrook was planned. If they took Baggotrath Castle, which was partly demolished to reduce its usefulness to them, they could then dig a trench to the Liffey, mount an artillery battery there and prevent further reinforcement by sea. Major-General Purcell took 1,500 foot and a detachment of 800 sappers down the hill sometime after midnight on 2 August. By dawn they had just managed to march the two miles to their objective and start digging. Jones was energetic in getting his men on the move, taking position south-east of Trinity College, probably along what is now Mount Street and around Merrion Square. Ormond contented himself with telling Purcell to dig like fury, standing the rest of his army to arms and then, fatigued by the night's tensions, he went to bed.

Jones advanced on Baggotrath with 1,200 horse and some 3,500 foot, hurling Ormond's cavalry aside and sending them running for Ballsbridge and the safety of the far bank of the River Dodder. Purcell's detachment was made of sterner stuff and held at Baggotrath until they were killed, wounded or captured. Ormond, aroused from his slumbers, joined the rest of his army at Ranelagh and placed two regiments on his right without any clear instructions; they were to await further orders. It was already too late, for Jones's horse had turned south along the Dodder, past Clonskea to Milltown and were now hooking back north to hit Ormond from the rear. At the same time Jones's infantry were advancing on the other side of them and, although they gave good account of themselves, the men of Ormond's centre were doomed. The remaining left wing, for the most part, were quick in removing themselves from harm. Only a few hung on defiantly, but within two hours of commencing action Jones had routed his enemies. He was, understandably, pleased, saying, 'Never was any day in Ireland like this, to the confusion of the Irish, and to the raising up spirits of the poor English ...' from which it is clear he had perceived himself seriously hard pressed before the fight.

Oliver Cromwell landed at Dublin on 15 August with 12,000 men, having sailed from Milford Haven and been thoroughly sick for most of the crossing. At College Green he spoke, bareheaded, from his carriage. According to the *Perfect Diurnall* of 23 August he declared he had come to restore liberty, property, happiness and tranquillity, and to propagate the Gospel of Christ. He spoke also of the 'barbarous and bloodthirsty Irish'. On 24 August he issued a declaration that began:

> Whereas I am informed that, upon the marching out of Armies heretofore, or of parties from Garrisons, a liberty hath been taken by the Soldiery to abuse, rob and pillage, and too often to execute cruelties upon the Country People: being resolved, by the grace of God, diligently and strictly to restrain such wickedness for the future.

> I do hereby warn and require all Officers, Soldiers and others under my command, henceforth to forbear all such evil practices as aforesaid; and not to do any wrong or violence toward Country People, or persons whatsoever, unless they be actually in arms or office with the Enemy ...

He went on to give assurance that supplies made to his army would be paid for and that, provided people registered with the appropriate authorities, they would be protected in their property and living.

Given the popular view of Cromwell's conduct in Ireland and recognising that a substantial number of people regard him, retrospectively, as an example of a war criminal (although that is a concept dating from 8 August 1945 when the London Agreement for the Prosecution and Punishment of the Major War Criminals of the European Axis was signed and which depended on conventions only half a century old) another aspect of war in the seventeenth century needs to be examined: the conduct of sieges. The Thirty Years' War had only ended in October 1648 and great tracts of Europe had been stripped and pillaged by starving and unpaid troops, numerous battles fought and cities taken. Many of the combatants in Ireland owed their skills to their experience in that war. Cromwell's declaration was, for a start, a signal advance on the rules accepted at the time, and the rules of siege were generally recognised as being the following:

On arrival at the town the attacker called on the defenders to surrender. This was termed the First Summons. It was usually rejected, but if not the defenders marched out with all their weapons and supplies and went away. If it was rejected, the attacker set about creating a blockade by digging trenches and so forth to prevent supplies going in. Once the blockade was complete, the Second Summons was issued. If accepted, stores were forfeit but the defenders could still take their weapons. Alternatively, a messenger could be sent for help and a month allowed for it to arrive, failing which the town would be yielded – the same sort of arrangement that brought Edward II's men to the relief of Stirling Castle and their defeat at Bannockburn. The attackers could now commence their bombardment. Once a viable breech was made or the month had expired, the Third Summons went in and defenders had the chance to quit without their weapons while civilians could go with their goods. At this stage matters were becoming very serious and often the military would yield the town, thus saving civilians, but hold on in the castle.

If the defenders withdrew to the citadel, another month of bombardment might take place before a Fourth Summons was given, but there was no Fifth. A point was arrived at when it was clear that the attackers could have the place only if they stormed it and that was bound to be a very bloody and painful affair. If the defenders refused to surrender the town after the Third Summons or the castle after the Fourth, the price for the attackers' success would be high indeed, and in this case the lives of the defeated defenders would be forfeit. Everyone understood this and while the distinction between defenders as such – men bearing arms – and civilians was recognised in theory, the risks following the adrenalin-rich experience of taking a town by storm endangered non-combatants as well. Further evidence comes from a letter the Duke of Wellington wrote to Canning on 3 February 1820, saying:

> I believe it has always been understood that the defenders of a fortress stormed have no claim to quarter [i.e. surrender]; and the practice which prevailed during the last century of surrendering a fortress when a breach was opened in the body of the place … was founded on this understanding.

By far the greater part of Drogheda stood north of the River Boyne and the smaller southern section around the mound known as Millmount (for it was surmounted by a windmill) was connected to it by a wooden drawbridge over the river. The eastern side of the Millmount enclosure was protected by a deep ditch and the Butter Gate at the north-western side of it was at the top of a slope. The Duleek Gate on the southern wall, west of St Mary's Church, was on the flat. Hills rose to the south where Cromwell and his army made their appearance on 3 September, the fleet sailing up the coast in support at the same time. The town was defended by a force under the one-legged Sir Arthur Aston who, according to the muster rolls dated 30 August, had 2,552 men at

Millmount, Drogheda, now crowned with an eighteenth-century fortification.

his disposal and, by the end of the siege, this could have increased to a little over 3,000 as a small number of reinforcements reached him. He had high hopes of getting more as Owen Roe O'Neill had finally decided to come in support of the royalists, but the great soldier was very ill and never made it; indeed he died on 6 November.

At eight o'clock on the morning of 10 September a letter was delivered to Aston. It read:

> Sir, having brought the army belonging to the Parliament of England before this place, to reduce it to obedience, to the end effusion of blood may be prevented, I thought it fit to summon you to deliver the same into my hands to their use. If this be refused, you will have no cause to blame me. I expect your answer and rest your servant, O. Cromwell.

Aston refused. The bombardment began. The power of the heavy guns was, perhaps, something of a surprise to Aston's men, for the siege undertaken by their own side in the person of Sir Phelim O'Neill at the close of 1641 had failed by March the following year with the walls unbreached. By the evening of the first day of this attack the damage was serious, with two small gaps made in the southern wall east of the Duleek Gate. Under cover of darkness the defenders toiled to make the damage good and continued through the next day to dig trenches within the walls. Three lines of earthworks were thrown up near St Mary's Church, to the Duleek Gate on one side and to the wall on the other. It was clear that they had no intention of yielding to a further summons from Cromwell.

All through the next day, 11 September, the bombardment continued. By about five o'clock the breaches were judged to be vulnerable to assault and three regiments of foot, some 600 men according to Cromwell, were ordered forward for the task. Colonel James Castle led the attack and was shot down in doing so. The musket fire from the entrenchments drove the Parliament men back out of the breach, but they rallied and returned to the assault only to be ejected once more. Nearby a tenalia – a defensive tower separated from the walls as such – stood in front of a sally port, the traces of which can be found today. Cromwell wrote to William Lenthall, Speaker of the House of Commons, on 17 September, saying:

> There was a tenalia to flanker the south wall of the town, between Duleek gate and the corner tower before mentioned [near St Mary's], which our men entered, wherein they found some forty or fifty of the enemy, which they put to the sword. And this they held, but it being without the wall, and the sally port through the wall into that tenalia being chocked up with some of the enemy that were killed in it, it proved of no use for our entrance into the town that way.

Bulstrode Whitlocke, writing perhaps as much as thirty years later, but possibly drawing on eyewitness accounts, said:

> ... the breaches, not being made low enough, the horse could not go in with the foot, but the foot alone stormed and entered the town, but by reason of

the numerousness and stoutness [courage] of the enemy, who maintained the breach as gallantly as ever men did ... our men were disheartened and retreated, which my Lord Lieutenant seeing, went himself ...

Cromwell had been standing by, mounted, and awaiting the opening of the Duleek Gate from within by his men. He now joined his troops on foot in a third effort. He would have seen what happened next with his own eyes, and wrote to Lenthall:

And after a very hot dispute, the enemy having both horse and foot and we only foot, within the wall, they gave ground and our men became masters both of their retrenchments and the church, which indeed, although they made our entrance more difficult, yet they proved of excellent use to us so that the enemy could not annoy us with their horse ...

The captured defences also helped Cromwell bring his own cavalry through the breaches, high though the remaining wall was. Of the sixty-four Commonwealth soldiers said to have been killed that day, it is probable almost all had met their

A vestige of Drogheda's city walls survives in the St Laurence Gate.

fate by this point and numerous others had been wounded. The storming had cost them over ten per cent in fatalities; they had literally been decimated.

Aston's men fell back, some with him to the Millmount, others towards the bridge and the northern half of the town. About 250 men held the daunting position on top of the great mound between the Duleek Gate and the bridge and, fearing the cost of yet another storming assault, Cromwell gave the order to put the defenders and all that were in arms in the town to the sword. Exactly how the Millmount fell is not clear but it certainly was not the result of a fight of any significance, for Commonwealth casualties would have been huge. Rather it seems that Aston and his men were duped into accepting an offer of quarter, a trick probably played on many others that day, and once they had surrendered their arms they were killed. The pursuit of those fleeing to the bridge was close, so close that the Royalists failed to raise the drawbridge and the chase continued into the northern half of the town. Into the West Gate and the round tower alongside St Sundays they ran, and some climbed into the tower of the church of St Peter's, off Magdalene Street. The men in St Peter's were summoned to surrender but did not. Cromwell wrote:

> ... I ordered the steeple of St Peter's church to be fired where one of them was heard to say in the midst of the flames, 'God damn me, God confound me, I burn, I burn.'

Other reports tell of an attempt to blow the steeple up with gunpowder, but it failed, destroying the body of the church.

The other fugitives were more fortunate, perhaps because they were not dealt with until the following day when tempers had cooled. The tower 'next the gate called St Sundays' was, it is suggested, the Tooting Tower which stood near the junction of the modern King Street with Magdalene Street and Scarlet Street. West Gate stood where West Street reached the town walls. There were about 200 men in these places and at first they declined to come down. From one of them (Cromwell does not specify which, but the historian Tom Reilly suggests the Tooting Tower) the Royalists fired and killed some of his men. When, finally, they surrendered, the officers and every tenth man were put to death, and the rest imprisoned, destined for transportation to the Barbados. About 250 Royalists from Drogheda were transported, so their slaughter was not quite as comprehensive as popular reports have it. As to civilians, five Catholic priests were killed and, according to Reilly, there is no contemporary evidence of anyone else not under arms being killed. The highest number of casualties credibly cited is 3,500 and the conservative estimate of the number of defenders is 3,000. The allegation that hundreds or even thousands of civilians were massacred is thus clearly mistaken.

The killing of the garrison at Drogheda was, in the short term, effective. Dundalk and Trim were surrendered without a fight and Cromwell returned to Dublin on his way to deal with the continuing resistance at Waterford, Wexford and other towns of the south-east.

The Williamite War

As the restoration of the monarchy in 1660 faded into memory, the tensions between Catholic and Protestant throughout Europe became manifest in political unrest that lies beyond the scope of this book. Equally the commercial wars between the Netherlands and England and the curious circumstance of Pope Innocent XI approving the fight of William of Orange (William III) against the dethroned James II are for another work. What matters for the present purpose is that the wars being waged by King Louis XIV of France spilled into Ireland.

In military affairs changes had taken place. In addition to the dragoon – a mounted infantryman able to move swiftly across country in order to fight on foot – there now appeared the mounted grenadier. John Evelyn recorded seeing grenadiers on 29 June 1678:

> Return'd with my Lord [Chamberlaine] by Hounslow Heath, where we saw the new-rais'd army encamp'd, design'd against France, in pretence at least but which gave umbrage to Parliament. His Majesty [Charles II] and a world of company were in the field, and the whole armie in battalia, a very glorious sight. Now were brought into service a new sort of Soldiers call'd Grenadiers, who were dextrous in flinging hand granados ... they had furr'd caps with coped crowns like Janizaries, which made them look very fierce ...

The mounted version of this new sort of soldier was introduced in England in 1683, according to G.A. Hayes-McCoy, and into Ireland the following year. The traditional cavalry remained part of the army and by now had adopted the tactics common by the time of the battle of Naseby of charging home with the sword instead of firing pistols from far off, which had worked well enough against opponents lacking firearms.

The most impressive change had been in the infantry. The pikemen were now very much in the minority and were used to defend the musketeers. The musketeers themselves had changed, the most up-to-date of them no longer being the handlers of the clumsy match-lock with its glowing match ignition system, but using fire-locks which used sparks from a flint to set off the gun-powder. Further, swords were now fixed to the musket to give the gunman a pike-like weapon. These bayonets, apparently a French invention, originally plugged into the gun barrel, which was fine if you did not want to shoot. By 1689 the bayonet had been developed to fit around the musket's muzzle, leaving a hole for shooting, but very few, if any, of these would have been available to the troops in Ireland.

Musketry tactics had also changed to increase the effect of volley fire. The usual arrangement was to have the musketeers in six ranks but instead of the front rank alone firing, as fifty years earlier, the lighter modern muskets permitted the front rank to crouch, the second to kneel and the third to stand and deliver a serious volley. They then hurried to the rear and the rear three ranks came forward to do likewise. The most modern of the muskets, the fusil, was a sixteen-bore in calibre, that is it took balls made to a size that gave sixteen of them for each pound of lead, and a paper cartridge including the bullet and the correct charge of powder was used. It was an immense improvement on earlier weapons. Behind them all the pikemen stood ready to move forward and deal with a cavalry attack.

In 1651 at the battle of Worcester Cromwell had made use of 'bridges of boats' to overcome the obstacle of the river and in his Irish expedition William of Orange had twenty 'tyn boates' in his artillery train; durable boats for use in constructing pontoon bridges.

In August 1689 the Williamite army of some 20,000 men had landed at Carrickfergus to support the resistance to the Jacobites successfully demonstrated at Enniskillen and Londonderry. Marshal Frederick Herman, Duke of Schomberg, was some seventy-five years of age and had been a serving soldier all his adult life, commanding Dutch, French and Portuguese forces in various wars. William of Orange recruited him for his invasion of England and the old man commanded the army sent to Ulster. Schomberg made a cautious advance southwards towards Dundalk before retiring for the winter to Lisburn. His force suffered from illness and deprivation through the winter, mainly because of the corruption that prevailed in the system of regimental supply. In March he was reinforced with a Danish army of 1,000 horse and 6,000 foot commanded by the German Duke of Würtemberg-Neustadt. More English and Dutch soldiers came in May and William of Orange himself came on 14 June. In all he had about 36,000 men: Irish, Dutch, Danish, French, German, Huguenot and even some English.

The Jacobite forces had passed the winter in Dublin and in March 5,387 Irishmen were exchanged for 7,000 French infantry under the Count de Lauzun. The Irish were to be the first of many to leave for service in the French army, soldiers who would become known as the Wild Geese. James II moved north from Dublin. One of his men, Captain John Stevens, said of the journey:

> Tuesday ye 20th [June] about 5 of the clock in the morning I returned to the Regiment and found them ready to march. It was ordered that neither officer nor souldier should quit the ranks, which was no small fatigue the weather being hot and the road excessively dusty, to that degree that we were also stifled and blinded, and so covered with dust we scarce knew ourselves ...

They marched eleven miles from Swords to Gormanston where they halted for two hours, but found no food or drink. Then on they went, first to Innistown and then on to Drogheda where they were quartered. Having arrived, he cheered up.

> ... All the country between this citie and Dublin is very pleasant, and a good soile, having great store of corn and some good pasture. The road in summer very good but in winter extreme deep unless helped by an old broken causeway, full of holes.

There were about 1,500 of James's men in Drogheda and his total force of some 25,000 prepared to oppose the Williamites on the River Boyne, the natural defence of the country north of Dublin.

The river itself is no puny thing. Not only is it broad, at times it is up to thirty yards (27.5m) wide and tidal. There were several well-known fords and the tides were predictable, but it was the obvious defensible line. It flows, here, west of Drogheda, in a zig-zag, running past Slane south-eastwards to Rosnaree before curving up north to a tight bend around what was the hamlet of Oldbridge (where no bridge stood at the time) before flowing east to the town. East of Rosnaree a small stream flowed north to the Boyne through boggy terrain with a wooded hill rising in the east and beyond it another hill on which stood the village of Donore. The north bank ran under a higher hill affording a good view in general, but it would have been clear that there was much opportunity for concealment in the little valleys and hollows. The next river to the south is the Nanny which, then, could only be crossed at Duleek.

James II made Donore his headquarters and had his infantry under the Earl of Tyrconnel before him at Oldbridge and along the river to the east. His cavalry was

Across the River Boyne from the north bank immediately to the east of Oldbridge. The level changed with the state of the tide and the receding waters permitted William's troops to cross further east as the day wore on.

to his rear at Plattin Hall, near the modern cement works. William of Orange arrived, having brought his army south both by way of the Moyry Pass, where they met some small opposition, and from Armagh. He made a reconnaissance on the evening of 30 June and narrowly escaped death when a ball from one of the Jacobite six-pounders took off the shoulder of his coat.

The conference William then held was divided in its opinion of how to proceed the next day. Schomberg was in favour of a flanking movement by the west at Rosnaree and a feint at Oldbridge while the next in seniority, Heinrich Maastricht, Count Solms-Braunfeld, a Dutch soldier, advocated a full frontal assault across the river at Oldbridge. Fortunately William had better sense than either of them and ordered Schomberg's son, Meinhard, to take a third of the army west early in the morning while he would use the rest of them on the Oldbridge to Drybridge, about halfway to Drogheda, sector.

In the mist of the morning of 1 July Meinhard's force crept away towards Slane, unobserved. Count de Lauzun, however, had advised James to make provision on his left and so Neil O'Neill had taken his dragoons, about 400 men, to keep an eye on the rivulet below Rosnaree. There the two forces clashed and though O'Neill

James camped near the old church of Donore from which he had a view across the valley of the Boyne to the hills north of the river where William had his headquarters.

The view south towards Rosnaree from north of the river. The Williamite forces crossed and advanced to the right of the river before wheeling left, to the east, in an attempt to take the Jacobites on the flank. On the hilltop to the extreme left is the prehistoric burial site of Knowth, and Newgrange lies a short distance to the south-east.

was greatly outnumbered, the terrain favoured defence and the Williamites could not make progress before, the alarm given, James was throwing in reinforcements. Patrick Sarsfield brought up his regiment, then another Jacobite unit arrived and de Lauzun came with the entire French force, six battalions of crack troops. Eventually more than 10,000 men were on the left flank. The attempt to take James on his left had been foiled and a third of William's army could do little more than stare at the Jacobites.

Meanwhile the tide was falling and the crossing at Oldbridge began. The mist had dispersed and the sun shone down cheerfully on the 6,000 men James had overlooking the river here. At about ten o'clock the crossing began with William's guns sending cannon balls over their heads towards Donore. Solms-Braunfeld sent the Dutch Guards in first, followed by the Huguenots and some English troops. James later wrote:

> ... the enemy ... attacked the regiment which was at the foot of Old Brig
> [Oldbridge] with a great body of foot, all strangers, and soon possessed
> themselves of it; upon which the seven battalions of the first line which
> were left there and drawn up a little behind the rising ground which
> sheltered them from the enemy's cannon marched up to charge them, and
> went on boldly till they came within a pike's length of the enemy,
> notwithstanding their perpetual fire, so that Major Arthur who was at the
> head of the first battalion of the Guards ran the officer through the body
> that commanded the battalion he marched up to.

On the Jacobite side the Irish Guards lost 150 men and the Dutch Guards lost
nearly as many in this first clash. Lord Tyrconnell's Irish cavalry came into
action against William's Blue Regiment of Foot Guards and, breaking through
them, turned on the Huguenots. They were led by Lord Caillemotte, who was
severely wounded and was carried back over the Boyne where he died.
Schomberg, seeing the Huguenots without a commander, rushed across the river
himself, only to be killed. The Jacobites were giving an excellent account of
themselves.

The tide was still going out and the next ford downstream became viable at
about eleven o'clock. The Duke of Würtemberg took the Danes, Sir John
Hanmer's, who were mainly Dutch, and Le Mellonière's brigades, over the river.
It was not easy, for the water was still high, perhaps shoulder deep for the
shorter men, and the bottom was muddy. The Danes were met only by a few
dragoons at first, and reinforcement from Oldbridge weakened that force,
allowing the Dutch Guards to make some ground at the scene of the earlier
crossing.

Still later, in the early afternoon, William found that the falling tide had made
the Drybridge ford possible to cross. He went over with the rest of his cavalry –
Dutch, Danish, English and the Ulstermen of the Enniskillen horse. To these last
William said, 'I have heard much of you. You shall be my guards, let me see
something of you.' He was not disappointed. James wrote:

> ... [our] horse did their duty with great bravery and tho' they did not break
> the enemy's foot it was more by reason of the ground's not being favourable
> than for want of vigour, for after they had been repulsed by the foot they
> rallied again and charged the enemy's horse and beat them every charge.

But he continues with a growing catalogue of the wounded and slain on his own
side, making his account of the effect, as opposed to the courage, of his troops
hard to credit. The Duke of Berwick, the natural son of James II, was over-ridden
and his Life Guards, originally 200 strong, reduced to only sixteen unwounded.
The Duke was rescued by a trooper and survived, but the undoubted bravery of
his men afforded no advantage. The Jacobites were forced back from the river
and up the hill, first to Donore and then to Duleek.

A view from the south of the river towards the north west over the scene of the hardest fighting opposite Oldbridge and King William's Glen on the far side.

Captain Stevens never got involved in the fighting. His regiment was ordered to support Neil O'Neill's, but as they moved forward the Jacobite cavalry was falling back from Oldbridge, riding clean through their ranks and scattering them. Stevens did his best to regain control, but:

> What few men I could see I called to, no commands being of force, begging them to stand together and repair to their colours, the danger being in dispersing, but all in vain, some throwing away their arms, others even their coats and shoes to run the lighter ...

Both wings of James's army retreated to Duleek and passed south across the River Nanny. The Williamites, exhausted by the hard contest, advanced to the village and no further. Even today the crossing is narrow, the river valley on either side is boggy and the hill to the south-east makes a handy artillery platform. James made for Dublin and soon after left for France. The remnants of his force went west, to Limerick, determined to fight another day.

The Birth of a Republic

The deployment of great forces and the clash of brave men in the field is not, in respect of events since 1700, easily illustrated in Dublin and the surrounding lands, save perhaps for the fight at the Hill of Tara in May 1798, where the United Irishmen's forces gathered. The rising of 1798 was organisationally flawed, the various controlling leaders being betrayed, dispersed or arrested, with the result that the uncoordinated outbreaks of rebellion, though serious, did not outstrip the British ability to suppress them. The *London Gazette* reported a communication from Dublin dated 15 May:

> The Lord Lieutenant and Privy Council of Ireland have issued a proclamation, declaring that they have received information upon oath, that Lord Edward Fitzgerald has been guilty of high treason, and offer a reward of 1000 sterling, to any person who shall discover, apprehend, or commit him to prison.

And then there was another report, dated 20 May, saying,

> Yesterday evening ... Mr Justice Swan, Major Sirr, and Captain Ryan, with a small guard, went in two coaches to the house of one Murphy, a feather-merchant, in Thomas-street. Major Sirr instantly proceeded to plant sentinels on the different doors of the house; Mr Swan and Captain Ryan rushed in, and ran up to a room two pair of stairs backwards. Mr Swan, having first reached the door, opened it, and told Lord Edward, who lay upon a bed in his dressing-gown and breeches, that he had a warrant against him.

Then, according to this report, followed a bloody, blundering brawl. Fitzgerald stabbed Swan and Swan shot at Fitzgerald before they wrestled one another, Swan getting another stab wound in the back in the process. Swan fell back, crying that he was killed, and Captain Ryan rushed in with his pocket pistol at the ready. It misfired, so Ryan drew his sword from his sword-stick and in striking at Lord Edward bent the weapon double. Lord Edward fell on the bed and Ryan threw himself on top of him and tried to hold him, receiving numerous stab wounds the while. Major Sirr raced towards the scene after the first shot and when he reached the room he put a round into Lord Edward's shoulder, at which point the man surrendered. The determined captain suffered fourteen stab wounds, and the June issue of the *Gentleman's Magazine* carried the following death announcement:

> At Dublin, in consequence of the wounds he received in assisting to apprehend Lord Edward Fitzgerald, Daniel-Frederick Ryan, esq. captain of the St. Sepulchre's corps.

On the next page of the same issue of the magazine appear the following words:

> At Dublin, in consequence of the wounds he received in the scuffle at his apprehension for high treason, Lord Edward Fitzgerald ...

In the Napoleonic wars the fear of French invasion led to the construction of Martello towers. This example is on the island known as Ireland's Eye, north of Howth and Dublin Bay. It was near Dublin, where they were least required, that the first examples were built.

This is augmented with a moving account of his final days and hours. Just below that, and of no direct relevance to these events but interesting none the less, is notice of the execution of Sir Edward Crosbie in Carlow, in consequence of his 'criminal intercourse with the rebel army'. The entry continues to point out that his brother, Richard, was the aeronaut who 'first ascended with a balloon in Ireland' and fell into the sea from which he had to be rescued. Sir Edward's head was set on a pike on Carlow markethouse.

The *London Gazette* extracts in the June 1798 issue of the *Gentleman's Magazine* cover a number of small fights in the environs of Dublin, including the Tara encounter. There a gathering of United Irishmen had been strengthened by the booty taken from a Scotch Fencible regiment. They took position on the hill, dug trenches and defied the local magnate, Lord Fingal, to attack them. The British report gives this version of events as contained in a letter from the Lord Lieutenant to London, dated 27 May:

> ... the body of rebels, who for some days had been in considerable force to the Northward of Dublin, were yesterday defeated, with a very great loss on their part, by a party of the Reay Fencibles, and the neighboring Yeomanry Corps, on the hill of Taragh ... Capt. Hill detached three of the companies under the command of Capt. M'Lean, with one field-piece, to the spot; who, being accompanied by Lord Fingal and his troop of Yeomanry, Capt. Preston's and the Lower Kells Yeomanry Cavalry, and Capt. Molloy's Company of Yeomanry Infantry, attacked the rebels, who, after some resistance, fled in all directions. Three hundred and fifty were found dead in the field this morning ... The loss on the part of the King's troops, was 9 rank and file killed, 16 wounded.

A little more information is given by Thomas Pakenham. He says the United forces, hundreds if not thousands strong, were deployed near the churchyard and that one Blanche (where the *Gazette* has M'Lean) led his tough little force up the hill to attack them. Things remained fairly evenly balanced until, thinking they were victorious, the insurgents rushed from behind their defences only to be destroyed by gunfire. He agrees that some 350 of them were killed but says the Fencibles suffered thirteen dead and twenty-eight wounded. The differences are details, but the details themselves can be revealing. The precise rehearsal of the King's forces involved was obviously a matter of importance to demonstrate one's loyalty and avoid the fate of poor Sir Edward Crosbie, whose adherence to his King in an earlier conflict could not redeem his error in a later one. The undisputed effect was to remove the threat of the United Irishmen.

In Dublin itself there have been more crucial conflicts. On Easter Monday, 24 April 1916, about 1,000 Irish Volunteers and some 200 Citizen Army, with perhaps another 600 Volunteers who joined before the action was over, occupied a number of locations within Dublin. The event was a surprise to the authorities not because it was unforeseen, but because it was considered so unwise that they could not believe it would happen. Indeed, it took place without even the approval of the highest ranks of the forces working for Irish independence, for although a scheme for a rising at some time before the end of the war had been hatched in August 1914, efforts to gain German support, raise an Irish Brigade amongst prisoners-of-war in Germany and import arms had been unsuccessful. On 9 April the *Aud*, a German ship disguised as Norwegian, sailed from Lübeck intending to make a landfall at Fenit, County Kerry, on Thursday, 20 April. She was due to meet with Sir Roger Casement who left Germany by submarine three days later. They missed each other. Casement and his companions were put ashore, and Sir Roger, whose intention was to prevent the rising taking place at that time, was caught. The *Aud* was apprehended by the British when sailing for home and was scuttled.

Eoin MacNeill, commander-in-chief of the Volunteers, was out-manoeuvred by the Irish Republican Brotherhood members of the Military Council, and at first, reluctantly, agreed to the idea of the Easter Rising which was to take place throughout the land. With the failure of the arms shipment to arrive and the capture of Casement, he ordered the abandonment of the project on the very eve of the event. On Easter Sunday Pádraig Pearse and his fellow-members of the Council conferred and, as a result, the order was sent secretly for the Dublin forces to assemble as previously planned, ensuring that the Easter Rising would take place as an isolated effort in that city alone, and thus fail.

The action began at noon on Easter Monday. The headquarters was established in the General Post Office with Pádraig Pearse as commander-in-chief and James Connolly, Commandant General of the Dublin District, in control. The position was in the shopping centre of the city, which was to suffer considerable damage in the following week. The Four Courts, the judicial centre of the city near the Liffey, was occupied by the Volunteers' 1st Battalion under Commandant Edward Daly, who set up posts at the Mendicity Institute, North Brunswick Street, Church Street and North King Street. South of the river, from west to east, the positions occupied were scattered and isolated from one another. The 4th Battalion was at South Dublin Union and Marrowbone Lane Distillery under the command of Eamon Ceannt. The 2nd Battalion under Thomas MacDonagh was to the south of Dublin Castle at Jacob's Biscuit Factory. Countess Markievicz and Michael Mallin had a mixed Volunteer and Citizen Army force at St Stephen's Green and the Royal College of Surgeons and, further east, the 3rd Battalion under Eamon de Valera was at Boland's Mills near Grand Canal Docks with outposts at Mount Street Bridge and Westland Row to Ringsend. Neither Dublin Castle nor Trinity College, both positions of greater strategic importance and credible as defensive positions, were subject to any serious attempt to take them; an impromptu force of college porters and soldiers on leave sufficed to defend the seat of learning. The object of the exercise appears to have been to attain a glorious defeat regardless of the consequences to individuals.

Boland's Flour Mills, in the canal basin, one of the positions occupied by the 3rd Battalion under Eamon de Valera in the Easter Rising.

The British troops in the Dublin area were few, perhaps some 2,500 men, and the extent of the Rising unclear to them. At about a quarter past one on Monday afternoon the 6th Reserve cavalry rode into O'Connell Street from the north and came under fire from the Post Office roof. Elsewhere there were a number of exchanges of shots as the British made tentative moves into the city, getting men into the Castle and into Trinity College, and some of the Volunteers' outposts were withdrawn. On Tuesday more men had arrived at the Post Office and the opportunity was taken to occupy nearby shops and hotels, in one of which a broadcasting station was set up by the Military Council to spread news of the conflict.

The British drew a cordon around the Four Courts and General Post Office north and south of the river, making the Castle and Trinity College their principal strengths, isolating the Volunteers to the south. On Tuesday four battalions of the Sherwood Foresters arrived from England and marched to the city as de Valera's men were occupying the railway line at Boland's Mills. The 7th and 8th Battalions met resistance at Mount Street Bridge, where de Valera had carefully positioned a mere seventeen men, and suffered about 230 casualties, some fatal. While pressure was kept up on all the Volunteers' positions, although only lightly on Boland's and Jacob's, the heaviest blows were directed at the headquarters in the Post Office which came under shellfire when guns arrived from Athlone. British soldiers were brought into the Amiens Street railway station without resistance, close to the action. The front of the Post Office was on fire by Friday afternoon and it was abandoned that evening. By Saturday afternoon Pearse was obliged to order unconditional surrender. About 450 people died. Of these, 64, including 16 later executed, were Volunteers, Citizen Army or their active supporters and 132 were members of the British armed forces. The rest were civilians. Another 2,500 or more from all groups were injured and massive damage had been done to the fabric of the city and the property of its citizens. The British reaction, for a country locked in the most punishing war it had ever experienced in Europe and the Middle East, was comparatively mild, but their oppressive measures were ill-judged.

The Four Courts became the focus of the dispute which developed into the Civil War in 1922. On 13 April that year the Dublin No. 1 Brigade occupied the buildings in an attempt to coerce the Dáil and the Irish Cabinet into repudiating the treaty intended to bring the Anglo-Irish War of 1919-1921 to an end. Many buildings were taken, but not the tactically important Four Courts Hotel; it belonged to Stephen O'Mara, Mayor of Limerick – not a person to insult. The occupation continued for weeks, with the British, who still had forces in Ireland, threatening to intervene and the new Irish Provisional Government in a terrible dilemma. Eventually, on 27 June, Michael Collins, possibly to prevent Winston Churchill ordering a British incursion, had the Dublin City Guard and the 2nd Eastern Division surround the area and at half past three the next morning the Republicans inside were given an ultimatum to evacuate. They did not and the attack began at a quarter past four. Two eighteen-pounder guns were lent by the British but made little impression on the stout buildings. Ammunition ran short, and the British supplied more but only had shrapnel to offer where high explosive shells were required. So poor was the work of the artillerymen that the British headquarters in Phoenix Park came under fire and the Irish had to apologise.

The two sides exchanged rifle fire to little purpose and Churchill even offered Collins aircraft, to be done up in Irish colours, with which to attack the position. There seems to have been little planning by the occupants before the fight and small command and control during it. The archives department had been used as the munitions centre and two mines had been laid there, presumably for use as a last resort. On 30 June they exploded, taking with them most of the contents of the Public Record Office and an immeasurable portion of Irish history. Fire swept through the buildings and the surviving Republicans were forced to surrender to the Free State forces. It was a messy, shameful start to a Civil War that was to be yet more costly than the conflict that had just ceased, and so painful in memory that historians have yet fully to analyse its causes and course.

The Four Courts, scene of fighting in the Easter Rising and of the disastrous explosion of 30 June 1922 at the outbreak of the Civil War.

2

The Achilles Heel of the South East

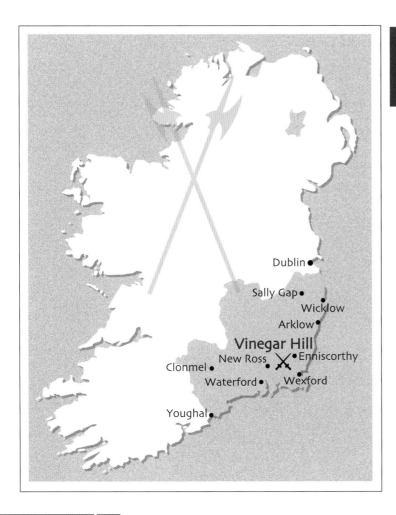

The land south of Dublin soon thins to a narrow, sea-side plain with the mountains of Wicklow rising to the west. It is easy to forget that they peak at over 3,000 feet (900m) and even today present a challenge to swift movement. In the far south east the lands fall along the line of the River Slaney and its tributaries on the way to Wexford. The Slaney cuts through the hills to the north, making an easy route towards Carlow and the midland plain. From Carlow the Barrow flows west of the Blackstairs Mountains due south through New Ross, where it is joined by the Nore from Kilkenny, and onwards to Waterford and the great estuary that makes so fine a

The Wicklow Mountains from the Military Road, south of Sally Gap.

haven. West of Waterford the Suir runs to the north of the Comeragh Mountains, through Clonmel, on its way down from Cahir, the Golden Vale and the valley below Cashel. From the sea, the viewpoint of the incomer, the south east offers a beguiling selection of routes into the centre of Ireland and to Dublin's western approaches.

The Incomers

The first of the incomers of the Christian era made little use of these opportunities, for the Vikings in the south east, as in Dublin, eventually ceased raiding and began trading. Wexford has its name from the Viking *Weisfjord*, a word that refers to the mud-flats formed of the silt of the Slaney. Ireland's first towns arose around the seaports and it was through these seaports that the Norman allies of Diarmaid MacMurchadha came to assist in his quarrel with Ruadhri Ó Conchobhair in 1169. Gerald of Wales tells of their arrival at Wexford, giving the impression, as was his wont, that the only people of note, other than the enemy, were Norman. Since they were there in Diarmaid's cause, fighting alongside his forces, that is clearly misleading, as is the idea that a Norman invasion was taking place. In early May 1169 Robert FitzStephen and his men arrived in three ships in Bannow Bay, on the south coast about halfway between Waterford and Wexford. He had thirty knights from his extended family, sixty men-at-arms and some three hundred archers from Wales. Messengers were sent to Diarmaid who sent his son, Domhnall, at once and came himself later with about 500 men. The combined force advanced on Wexford and the citizens of that place came out to oppose them, some 2,000 strong. One look at the Norman-Irish was enough; their unusual formation and the gleam and glamour of the knights' accoutrements filled them with alarm. The men of Wexford adopted scorched earth tactics, setting fire to outlying buildings and retiring behind the walls.

FitzStephen's force prepared to storm the town under the covering fire of archers, but when they rushed the walls a torrent of stones and baulks of timber showered down. One knight, Robert de Barry, was hit by a great stone on his helmet and was pulled from the ditch by his men. (The story goes that, eighteen years later, the blow caused his molars to drop out but new teeth immediately grew to replace them.) The attackers then set fire to what boats they could find in the harbour and attempted to take a cargo vessel filled with wine and wheat. The ship drifted out to sea and it was with difficulty that the attackers rowed ashore.

The next day a more considered approach to the town walls was made, but the citizens had also been thinking. The dangers of bringing matters to a point at which attackers had to storm a town were known to everyone, and the consequences were unattractive. Negotiations began and peace was soon made. FitzStephen and Maurice FitzGerald were granted Wexford by Diarmaid and their companion Hervey of Montmorency was given the lands along the seashore to the west as far as Waterford.

With their base established and their manpower augmented with Wexford men, they

A centaur portrayed as a Norman soldier with a conical helmet, bow and arrow above the north door, Cormac's Chapel, Cashel, County Tipperary. The lion symbolises the Celtic Christian church under attack from supporters of the Roman tradition.

turned their attention to Osraighe (Ossory), the region around modern Kilkenny. Domhnall, prince of Osraighe, had blinded Diarmaid's son as a crowning cruelty to his rebellion against MacMurchadha. It is not clear where the adversaries met, but Gerald of Wales says the terrain was restricted, wooded and boggy, which does not sound like the country of the River Barrow, but more like the route north-west from Enniscorthy. The Normans now put a well-tested tactic to use – the false retreat. It is said that the housecarls (household warriors) fighting for Harold against William the Bastard at Hastings were fooled by just such a ruse. FitzStephen's knights turned and, apparently, fled. Domhnall's men chased after them enthusiastically, pursuing them right out onto the plain and there, in open country well-suited to mounted men, they were slain. The Irish foot joined in with battle-axes and two hundred severed heads were presented to Diarmaid MacMurchadha. Gerald's ideas of typical Irish behaviour were then given rein, and as he did not visit Ireland until 1183, this account must be based on reports or gossip.

> When he [Diarmaid] had turned each one over and recognised it, out of an excess of joy he jumped three times in the air with arms clasped over his head, and joyfully gave thanks to the Supreme Creator as he loudly revelled in his triumph. He lifted up to his mouth the head of one he particularly loathed, and taking it by the ears and hair, gnawed at the nose and cheeks ...

Waterford: the Watch Gate and the city walls.

The following year the campaign continued, with Raymond le Gros preceding Richard de Clare (Strongbow), to Ireland from Wales. Le Gros arrived in May with a small force of ten knights and seventy archers, landing near Waterford, according to Gerald, at a place called Dundunnolf, which he says is four miles from Waterford and south of Wexford. They built themselves a rudimentary fort of branches and earth. The citizens of Waterford, said to number about 3,000 men, under Máelsechlainn Ua Fáeláin, came over the River Suir to attack them. The Normans received the assault in front of their defence lines and were forced to retreat, vigorously followed by their enemies. Raymond himself turned to hold the entrance and, with a great cry, thrust his sword through the first man to attempt to pass. The Waterford force lost enthusiasm for the fight and turned to flee. The pursuers became the pursued and Gerald claims 500 were slain by his valiant kinsman and yet more were thrown off the cliffs into the sea. The prize of Waterford was not attained. About seventy of the Ostmen and Irish had been taken prisoner, but instead of trading them for the city, Raymond had them executed, breaking their limbs and casting them off the cliffs to drown.

Strongbow himself arrived in August with 200 knights and about 1,000 other soldiers. Waterford was attacked again and twice the Normans were thrown back from the walls. Eventually a breach was made and they swarmed in, slashing and killing without distinction. Here Strongbow collected his prize; he was married as promised to Diarmaid MacMurchadha's daughter Aoife. It is said that the hem of her gown was soaked with blood.

After the taking of Dublin, the death of Diarmaid and the successful defence of the city, Strongbow claimed the vacant throne of Leinster. Not everyone was content with this and Robert FitzStephen was attacked in Wexford and made prisoner by the Ostmen. Henry II intervened, for Strongbow was meant to be his man and was now setting up a personal fief on the king's doorstep. The erring vassal made his peace and Henry journeyed to Ireland, landing at Waterford on 17 October 1171. Here the Ostmen offered to give him FitzStephen, bringing him before the king in chains. After a severe telling-off, FitzStephen was committed to Raghnall's Tower, chained to another man. Henry accepted the fealty of the king of Cork, also called Diarmaid, and then, moving to Cashel, extended his protection to Domhnall, king of Limerick. A satisfying journey continued with lord and king alike, with the sole exception of Ruadhri Ó Conchobhair, accepting Henry as their ruler. This had the effect of obliging Henry to maintain the peace and, as Strongbow was in exactly the same position as the Irish kings, keeping the Normans in their place. Finally Henry returned to Waterford and had FitzStephen brought before him and pardoned him, but although he was granted his freedom he did not regain the lordship of Wexford.

Once the Normans were in, there was no getting them out. Just as they had in England, they extended their territorial hold and kept it in place with the construction of castles. At first these were simple mottes, artificial earthen mounds crowned with a palisade forming a primitive defensive position sufficient to repel the yet more primitive techniques of the warriors they faced. Like all such forts, they had

Mail-clad Norman knights, known as The Brethren, in the southern chapel, Jerpoint Abbey, County Kilkenny.

A superb carving of a Norman knight, known as the Cantwell Effigy, at Kilfane Church, County Kilkenny. His mail, shield and spurs are beautifully shown.

the great weakness of being hard to quit in the face of opposition, so to sally forth to take the fight to the enemy was a dangerous business. The addition of a bailey, an enclosure surrounding the motte, not only secured supporting buildings and supplies, but made an unexpected exit harder to monitor. The location of mottes shows how the Normans spread along the rivers to New Ross, Kells and Kilkenny, to Carlow and Athy, along the Suir to Carrick and through to Limerick and up the east coast past Enniscorthy. Then they built in stone, often using the old motte as their starting point. The purpose was, as in England, to dominate. The mass and might of the castle was intended to convey the strength and solidity of their hold on the land, and to some extent it worked. The Irish, however, were less respectful of foreign masters than most. Equally the incomers steadily became residents, growing closer to their Irish neighbours and further from their supposed superiors in England.

The view from England altered also as the Hundred Years' War and the Wars of the Roses pressed more immediately on the attention of London-based monarchs. The English influence was rolled back until, in 1366, as an attempt to preserve what was left, Edward III had the Statutes of Kilkenny enacted forbidding his English subjects getting too close to their Gaelic neighbours. In church affairs it had some success, but in social and political matters it was largely a dead letter. Richard II was the first English monarch to actually visit Ireland since John. He brought a substantial army

Black Castle, protecting the harbour at Wicklow. It was built in 1176 by Maurice FitzGerald.

Caher Castle was built on an island in the River Suir to hold the strategically important crossing. Most of what survives dates from the fifteenth century, for the place was held and improved over many years.

in his campaign of 1394–95 and managed to renew the declarations of loyalty by the Irish lords. In the south east he used the castles as centres for a series of forays against Art MacMurrough, whom the English commentators of the day were careful to call 'chief of Leinster' rather than 'king', and against O'Byrne and O'Nolan. The unhesitating use of superior force prevailed against the traditional mountain-based, hit-and-run tactics only while large numbers of well-funded men in the English service were available. After Richard left, this situation endured for a while before the usual benign neglect resumed and inter-chieftain rivalry was once more the norm.

Cromwell's Campaign

The south east was spared much of the turmoil that marked the late middle ages and the Elizabethan age elsewhere in Ireland. The fear of the offshore island being used as a springboard for an attack on Britain had its impact in Ulster and Munster but not here. The aftermath of the English Civil War and the 1641 Rising in Ireland, unfortunately, had disastrous consequences for the south east.

In an attack more notorious than the facts support, Oliver Cromwell, appointed Lord Lieutenant of Ireland by an English Parliament, took Drogheda on 11 September 1649, as described in chapter one. Dundalk and Trim capitulated without argument. He then came south to deal with the principal lines of supply the Royalists were using through Wexford and Waterford. Wexford had been strong in the Catholic cause in 1641 and in January the next year an order was issued by Viscount Mountgarret to all Protestants, instructing them to leave the place. Of eighty who attempted to do so by ship, only one survived when the vessel foundered. What was even more offensive to the Lord Lieutenant was the town's deserved reputation as a centre of piracy, or, if one viewed the matter through Confederate eyes, privateering. The result was an enclave of prosperity in the south east of a country generally in great need. Cromwell saw Wexford as rich, rebellious and actively supplying his enemies, and could have had no hesitation in marking the town as his next conquest.

On 28 September the Cromwellian army was at Arklow, on the coast south of Wicklow. The town surrendered. The advance continued by way of Rosseminoge Castle at Slane Passage, Limbrick and Enniscorthy, with a number of skirmishes fought as they went. The fleet was following and arrived outside Wexford on 29 September, but, as the fort of Rosslare was in Royalist hands, could not enter the harbour itself. The army, now numbering about 9,000 men, arrived on 1 and 2 October and camped at the north-west corner of the town. They were opposed by the garrison of Wexford which included those mariners, or as Cromwell might have it, pirates, currently in port and the Catholic citizenry who had been so keen on the Confederation. In command was one Colonel David Sinnott, appointed by the Earl of Castlehaven to whom the other Lord Lieutenant, the Royalist, Protestant Earl of Ormond, had entrusted the defence of the south east. The townsmen of Wexford were not impressed with Sinnott, nor he with them. He wrote to Ormond on 30 September, saying that he feared they would yield the place up to Cromwell.

> ... seeing I am not able to do H[is] M[ajesty] any service I am resolved to leave the town without I find their undelayed conformity, all which out of my duty, I humbly offer your Excellency and assure your Lordship that the place will be lost to H. M. without your Excellency's interpost H. M.'s forces for the defence thereof, which if sene by the towne will incourage them and nothing else as I conceave such impression they have of Drogheda ...

In response to this an ambitious plan was made to relieve the town by attacking Cromwell where he stood on the shore across the Slaney from Wexford. Sinnott was to be directed to send spies into the Commonwealth camp and see how best it might be assaulted. A force of 1,000 horse and 2,000 foot was then to be deployed in a number of special units, false alarms were to be given, raiders used and an eventual victory to be achieved in accordance with the detailed description of the author. It was the wildest fiction and an entirely unrealistic response to the crisis. It was a woeful failure given that the enemy were also facing difficulties.

Cromwell needed to hasten his attack, for the October weather was uncomfortably wet and windy and the troops were starting to become ill; dysentery was the worst problem. His heavy guns were still at sea and he was on the wrong side of the river. On 2 October Colonel Jones was sent to deal with the fort at Rosslare, with unexpected speed, for, as one Hugh Peters wrote the next day:

Wexford, seen across the River Slaney and the harbour.

> Yesterday we tooke in the Forte here before Wexford which commanded their harbour, which is now become ours. They fled into a Frigot which lay close by their Fort which our ships had chased in. They also took the Frigot, a new vessel of the Lord of Antryms, with fourteen guns in her. The fort had seven guns ... They have put 1500 men into the towne where there were 2000 before. Here is a very good country. We want nothing more but men to possess it.

With the fort secured without resistance, Cromwell was free to move. He established himself to the south of the town on an outcrop called Trespan Rocks, above modern Maudlinstown, with a view of the town walls and the castle of Wexford which stood outside the walls themselves.

The 1,500 men put into the town were Sinnott's troops and now Ormond had acquired another 1,300 which were being sent towards Wexford. Cromwell had no time to waste and, on 3 October, summoned the town to surrender as follows:

> Sir, Having brought the army belonging to the Parliament of England before this place, to reduce it to obedience, to the end effusion of blood may be prevented and the town and the country about it preserved from ruin, I thought it fit to summon you to deliver the same to me, to the use of the State of England. By this offer, I hope it will clearly appear where the guilt will lie, if innocent persons should come to suffer with the nocent. I expect your speedy answer; and rest, Sir, your servant, O. Cromwell.

It should be noted that the order Cromwell gave at the start of his campaign – that non-combatants should not be harmed – was still in force and the reference to innocent persons is as likely to mean they risked the loss of their houses and property as meaning they might get killed by unruly soldiers.

Colonel Sinnott played for time. He wrote to say he had to discuss the matter with his military colleagues and the Mayor of the town and he promised a reply by noon the next day. The citizens went so far as to send a cart loaded with 'sack [sherry], strong waters and strong beer' to Cromwell, presumably to ingratiate themselves with him in the face of possible military defiance. The formal reply came, as agreed, on 4 October.

> Sir, I have advised with the Mayor and officers, as I promised; and I am content that four whom I shall employ, may have a conference with four of yours, to see if any agreement may be begot between us ... And I pray that the meeting may be had to-morrow at eight in the forenoon ...

Cromwell's response was firm.

> Sir, Having summoned you to deliver the town of Wexford into my hands, I might well expect the delivery thereof, and not a formal treaty; which is seldom granted but where things stand upon a more equal foot.

> If, therefore, yourself or the town have any desires to offer, upon which you will surrender the place to me, I shall be able to judge of the reasonableness of them when they are made to me. To which end, if you shall see fit to send the persons named in your last [letter], intrusted by yourself and the town ... I shall give you a speedy and fitting answer, and I do hereby engage myself that they shall return in safety to you. I expect your answer hereunto within an hour; and rest your servant, O. Cromwell.

Both sides were busy with other things while this correspondence was conducted. Cromwell was preparing his gun positions and Colonel Sinnott strengthening the defences and dragging out time in the hope of getting the Earl of Ormond to send in reinforcements. Sinnott rushed a reply to Cromwell proposing a meeting with his envoys at eight the next morning and on 5 October this was followed with another letter saying his men were ready to come if Cromwell sent a safe conduct back by the same messenger. That same day the Earl of Castlehaven, who outranked Sinnott, arrived on the other side of town with the expected reinforcements, 1,500 men of Lord Iveagh's Ulster Regiment. Sinnott made his excuses to Cromwell, explaining that he now had to have the approval of his superior officer and could not proceed until that was obtained. At the same time he wrote to the Earl of Ormond to welcome the help and ask for more as he was too weak to send out parties to cover the entry of the new force.

Cromwell wrote to Colonel Sinnott to revoke the safe conduct given the previous day and to express his lack of interest in Sinnott's reasons for the delay, but he left the way open for a meeting if the Royalists wanted one. On 8 October Ormond himself, with another 3,000 men, reached Ferrybank, opposite the town, and wrote to Sinnott on 9 October at 9 a.m. promising support. Another letter, dated 9 October from Farralstown, to the Mayor of Wexford, promises the supply of their needs but, as supplies are short, asks for the 'unnecessary people, as ould men, women and children' to be sent out of the town. Evidently a prolonged resistance was contemplated, in spite of the appearance of negotiations with Cromwell. The Commonwealth headquarters had been established at what is now known as Cromwell's Fort on the high ground south of the town and, by the evening of 10 October, a four-gun battery was ready to engage the castle. The bombardment was ordered early the next day and by dawn two breaches had been made in its walls. Sinnott's request for a safe conduct for his negotiators reached Cromwell before noon.

The demands made showed little understanding of either the extreme danger Wexford was now in or the deeply-held convictions of the Puritans with whom they were attempting to deal. The ten resolutions asked, in short, that in exchange for a formal surrender the garrison should be allowed to depart fully armed and that the business of the inhabitants, including the privateers, should continue and any past offences should be pardoned. Above all, the position and conduct of the Catholic church should persist unaffected. Cromwell answered:

> Sir, I have had the patience to peruse your propositions; to which I might have returned an answer with some disdain. But, to be short, I shall give the soldiers and non commissioned officers quarter for life and leave to go to their several habitations, with their wearing clothes; they engaging themselves to take up arms no more with [against] the Parliament of England; and the commissioned officers for their lives, but to render themselves prisoners. And as for the inhabitants, I shall engage myself that no violence shall be offered to their goods and that I shall protect their town from plunder ...

He gave them an hour to answer. It appears that the letter was never received by Sinnott, for events at the castle intervened and the confusion that reigned at the time clouds attempts at interpretation today.

The castle was commanded by Captain James Stafford who had also been one of the delegates to Cromwell and who himself recounted the events as follows:

> Upon Thursday the 11th instant (our batteries being finished the night before) we began to play betimes in the morning, and having spent near a hundred shot, the Governor's stomach came down, and he sent to me to give leave for four persons intrusted by him to come unto me, and offer terms of surrender, which I condescending to, two field officers, with an Alderman of the town and a captain of the castle, brought out the propositions enclosed,

which for their abominableness, manifesting also the impudency of the men, I thought fit to present to your view, together with my answer, which indeed had no effect. For whilst I was preparing of it, studying to preserve the town from plunder, that it might be of the more use to you and your army, the captain, being one of the commissioners, being fairly treated, yielded up the castle to us, upon the top of which our men no sooner appeared, but the enemy quitted the walls of the town ...

There are other versions. It has been said Captain Stafford was tricked into surrender and he has also been accused of treachery. Quite how the news was conveyed to the men surrounding the castle is unclear, assuming Stafford was still at Cromwell's headquarters. What is clear is that the appearance of the Commonwealth troops on the castle and the prospect of guns being brought to bear on them from that eminence caused the defenders of the walls abruptly to abandon their positions. A contemporary report quoted in Hore's history of the town said:

> ... they ran away from their walls on that side that was toward the Castle, quitted their guards, and betooke themselves towards their boats (whereof they had abundance belonging to their ships at their Keys within their Haven) which many of our souldiers from the Castle and some higher ground perceiving, they fell on their own accords, first without ladders, lifting and helping one another with their Pikes or any other way over the walls, and after with ladders, till they were got in a good number into the Towne, and then the enemy made head and got heart againe and attempting to have returned to their guards and walls we soon beat and dispersed them, and possessed the Towne ...

The Commonwealth troops were acting on their own rather than under direct orders from their General and the formal exchange of summonses and answers pertaining to a siege was broken without having come to a conclusion. A fight within the town followed while those who could made their escape by boat. Anyone bearing arms was considered fair game and killed. The streets had been 'gabled', that is blocked up with rope or baulks of timber, to inconvenience the cavalry but the infantry ducked through and many of the defenders were brought to bay in the Bull Ring, the market place. There they died. Any Catholic priest showing himself was slaughtered out of hand. There is no contemporary evidence of wanton killing of civilians, though the creation of tales of horror would, as in the case of Drogheda, become a feature of efforts to extract recompense from the king after the Restoration and such stories would be elaborated as time passed. The killed numbered 1,500 and the rest, the majority, got away. Colonel Sinnott was shot as he swam for safety and a number of boats were so overloaded with fugitives that they sank, taking civilians with them. The town fell in an hour, but it was nightfall before the depredations of the soldiery were finished, leaving the houses ruined and their contents smashed. Cromwell's chief regret appears to have been at the loss of comfortable winter quarters.

It was now clear that Cromwell was determined to subjugate the country and, while he might be reasonable and fair to those who surrendered, he was not likely to extend

The confluence of the rivers Suir and Barrow east of Waterford and south of New Ross. Access to the country to the west depended on having control of New Ross and the bridge there.

mercy to those who did not. On 17 October he was in front of the strategically important river crossing at New Ross. He wrote to the commander demanding surrender. It was not until the guns had started to destroy his defences on 19 October that the governor, Sir Lucas Taafe, replied, indicating his readiness to agree to 'conditions that may be safe and honourable for me to accept of'. Cromwell responded with an offer to allow the garrison to leave with arms, bag and baggage and with drums and colours and gave an undertaking that the inhabitants should be free of injury or violence. The bombardment, however, continued. A breach was made near Bewly Gate, now known as Three Bullet Gate, and a unit lined up ready to assault. Taafe was stimulated to write:

> ... I would propose ... such townsmen as have a desire to depart may have liberty ... to carry away themselves and their goods; and liberty of conscience to such as shall stay; and that I may carry away ... artillery and ammunition ...

The request for liberty of conscience was a sticking point for Cromwell. He told Taafe he had to leave such artillery and ammunition as he found when he arrived, and went on to say:

> For that which you mention concerning liberty of conscience, I meddle not with

Three Bullet Gate, New Ross. The walls nearby were breached by Cromwell's guns.

any man's conscience. But if ... you mean the liberty to exercise the Mass, I judge
it best to use plain dealing, and to let you know where the parliament of England
have power, that you will not be allowed of ...

The townsmen were allowed three months to leave if they wished to do so. Taafe
accepted. The Commonwealth forces moved into town and began the rebuilding of the
bridge. Obviously there was some foraging going on, for on 27 October Cromwell issued
a proclamation calling on his officers to prevent such outrages and to punish the
offenders they caught, that is, hang them. He was to issue a similar order on 8 December
when his cavalry were living off the country near Youghal. The army's progress was now
hampered by increasing disease, probably dysentery, and the attempts to take
Duncannon Fort and Waterford were abandoned on 5 November and 2 December
respectively. Cork had capitulated without even being approached, so Waterford could
be ignored for the time being.

In the new year Cromwell's progress continued until, on 27 April 1650, he came to
Clonmel, a walled Norman town on the River Suir. The town was held by Aodh Dubh
(Hugh Duff) O'Neill with 1,500 men and about 100 horse under a Major Fennell,
supported by a loyal populace. The summons to yield was rejected and the
Parliamentarian cannon were arrayed on Gallows Hill, north of the town, and
bombardment commenced. The efforts made by the attackers to enter the town were
repulsed while O'Neill's Ulstermen mounted sally after sally to molest their enemies. By

mid-May there had been made a large breach in the north wall close to the North Gate, which was on modern Gladstone Street below Morton Street. O'Neill expected the assault to come the next day. An account not contemporary, but written some thirty-five years later, published as *History of the War in Ireland from 1641 to 1653*, and not entirely reliable, says:

> ... Hugh ... did set all men and maids to work, townsmen and soldiers, only those on duty attending the breach and walls, to draw dunghills, mortar, stones and timber, and made a long lane a man's height and about eighty yards in length on both sides up from the breach, with a foot bank at the back of it; and caused to be placed engines on both sides of the same, and two guns at the end of it, invisible opposite the breach, and so ordered all things against a storm.

> Which storm was about eight o'clock in the morning ... and the English entered without any opposition; and there were but few to be seen in the town till they so entered, and the lane was crammed full of horsemen armed with helmets, back breast swords, musquetoons and pistols. On which those in the front seeing themselves in a pound, and could not make their way further, cried out, 'Halt! Halt!'

Those behind pushed on and soon the cul-de-sac was brimful of Cromwell's men. Then O'Neill's men moved, blocking off the entrance with pikemen and musketeers while from the sides and end of the confined space the guns opened fire, pistols were discharged, pikes stabbed and any missile the defenders could lay hands on was brought into play. The chronicler claims that, within an hour, all fell quiet with a thousand dead heaped in the trap. The attackers had to withdraw from the walls and Cromwell was forced to recognise that he had suffered a defeat that day.

After about five weeks' siege it became clear to Aodh Dubh O'Neill that ammunition was running low, supplies were close to exhaustion and the men worn out. Arrangements had to be made for the safe withdrawal of the fighting men from the town. O'Neill spoke to the Mayor, a man called John White, and got him to agree to negotiate with Cromwell. That night White, with a few followers, got away secretly over the river and rode to Waterford from where he sent a message to Cromwell asking for a meeting. A surrender was negotiated. *The History of the War* relates:

> After which Cromwell asked him if ... O'Neill knew of his coming out, to which he answered he did not, for that he was gone two hours after night fell with all his men, at which Cromwell stared and frowned at him and said, 'You knave you have served me so and did not tell me so before.' To which the Mayor replied that if his Excellency had demanded the question, he would tell him ...

> Then the Mayor delivered the keys of the gates to Cromwell who immediately commanded guards on them and next morning himself entered where he saw his men who had been killed in the pound, notwithstanding which and his fury that Hugh Duff went off as he did, he kept his conditions with the town.

Now affairs in Scotland drew the attention of the English Parliament and Cromwell was recalled. On 29 May he sailed from Youghal for England, leaving the final phase of the campaign in the hands of his son-in-law, Henry Ireton.

The 1798 Rising

Since the Middle Ages England had feared that Ireland would be the base from which invaders might come, be they Spanish or French. The French king had supplied James II with troops in the Williamite War but now, at the end of the eighteenth century, the king's executioners were the threat, and there were Irishmen keen to exploit their aid. It was not only in Europe that the cause of freedom and the rejection of monarchy had caught hold; the same was the case in the Americas. In Ireland the movement that gave expression to ideas of this kind was called the Society of United Irishmen. It was founded in Belfast on 18 October 1791 by a young lawyer, Theobald Wolfe Tone, and an army officer, Thomas Russell, as a Catholic/Protestant alliance for Irish self-rule. Tone was compromised by the Reverend William Jackson, a Church of Ireland clergyman, who was sent by the French in April 1795 to sound out the opportunities for a French-sponsored rising against the British. Tone agreed to exile in the USA and from there went to France himself to get backing for a rebellion. In 1796 he was in one of the ships that made the abortive attempt at a landing in Bantry Bay.

The threat of a French invasion put a mighty fear in the hearts both of the English in England and the Anglo-Protestant community in Ireland. The defence of the western flank of Britain was crucial in the war against France and the passions aroused by thoughts of freedom on the Irish side and thoughts of defeat on the English can easily be imagined. The response was the formation of the Yeomanry in 1796, forces that could only be deployed in their own localities and manned mainly by Protestants of the land-owning class, naturally antipathetic to the Catholic peasantry. In addition, making up a total military strength of some 80,000 men in Ireland, were the Militiamen, 23,000 mainly Catholic men officered by Protestants, and the Fencibles. The Fencibles were regular soldiers enlisted for service within the British Isles for the duration of the war. They gave the administration of Lord Camden about 8,000 cavalry, 13,000 infantry and 1,500 artillerymen of no particular political or religious bias; in effect they were just national servicemen doing what they were obliged to do and, no doubt, with the dour disinterest of most conscripts. What is more, as largely uneducated Scots or Englishmen, they had no sympathy with or interest in the Irish.

After a series of incidents, some involving the killing of various gentlemen and magistrates in ways that led to lurid accounts in the press, matters came to a head. On 30 March all Ireland was declared to be under the Insurrection Act; it was assumed the rebellion had begun. As a result, it had to be put down. General Sir Ralph Abercromby, who had made the mistake of speaking the truth about the army's atrocious conduct and ordering it to cease, had been forced to resign. The man who had dealt so harshly with the supposed insurgents in Ulster, General

Gerard Lake, was now given command of the whole. Homes were burned and innocent people flogged in the search for rebels and armaments. In County Wicklow, for example, Mary Leadbeater wrote:

> To the Tyrone Militia were now added the Suffolk Fencibles. And the Ancient Britons [Welsh Fencibles], dressed in blue with much silver lace – a very pretty dress – came from Athy, seized the smiths' tools to prevent them from making pikes, and made prisoners of the smiths themselves. I could not see without emotion poor Owen Finn and his brother, handcuffed and weeping as they walked after the car containing those implements of industry which had enabled them to provide comfortably for the family. Several of them were whipped publicly to extort confessions about the pikes. The torture was excessive and the victims were long in recovering; and in almost every case it was applied fruitlessly ...

The news of the rising in Wexford reached Dublin on 28 May and Lord Camden wrote to London at 4 p.m.:

> ... intelligence has been received that the insurrection is spreading Southward; and it has broke out in great force in the County of Wexford ... the rebels in that quarter have assembled in such force that they have cut off a party of 100 men of the North Cork militia, who were sent to meet them. Col. Foote, who has returned to Wexford, states the number of the rebels to be at least 4,000, and a great number of them mounted ...

The letter was held until 9 p.m. lest there be more news, but there was not. Camden enclosed a copy of the exhortation published by the Roman Catholic authorities urging their flock to desist from rebellion.

In County Wexford the local clergy had good cause to believe that only by taking up arms against the excesses of lawful authority had their flocks any hope of survival. Reports, many probably exaggerated, but sufficient entirely true, of atrocities committed by the soldiers against the citizens were abundant. Father John Murphy of Boulavogue and Father Michael Murphy of Ballycanew, villages south of Gorey on the road to Wexford, were men who had been trying to maintain a proper respect for the government. Now, on Saturday 26 May, Father John was persuaded his people had to resist and they seized the arms stored at Lord Mountnorris's house at Camolin on the Enniscorthy road. The countryside was soon ablaze with Protestant houses fired by rebels and Catholic houses lit up by the yeomanry. By Sunday afternoon Father John and his band were ensconced on Oulart Hill, south of Boulavogue, and the alarm had reached Wexford from which Foote's men, North Cork Militia, were marching. The militia paused for refreshment on the way and were not entirely sober when they sighted the rebels on the hill.

What happened exactly is hard to tell. Colonel Foote reported that his second-in-command, a Major Lombard, gave an order to his 100 or so militia to attack the

United Irishmen carrying their fearsome pikes; a sculpture by Eamonn O'Doherty on the Wexford to New Ross road.

mass of between 500 and 1,000 insurgents without Foote's permission or approval. The puny force was annihilated. A surviving rebel stated, long after, that Foote was beguiled into a trap and his force destroyed. In all events the result was the same – the soldiers were wiped out, only four, including Foote, returning to Wexford. Panic ensued throughout the county.

On Monday the rebels, Father John Murphy's force from Oulart uniting with Father Michael's from Ballycanew, entered Ferns and on that day Captain Snowe organised the defences of Enniscorthy, placing his 300 or so men of the yeomanry and militia north west and south east at the entries to the town. The rebels came from the north east in vast numbers and, with panicked cattle and horses galloping in front of them, overwhelmed the garrison. Street fighting followed and Snowe did his best to concentrate his forces against the incursion, but his men were too few and too inexperienced to stay the tide. Enniscorthy burned.

Lieutenant-Colonel Jonas Watson was determined that such should not be the fate of Wexford town. Thatch was pulled off roofs and bakers forbidden to light their ovens. The medieval gateways were blocked up and loyal citizens furnished with muskets to supplement the 1,000-strong garrison. What was more, General Sir William Fawcett was on his way with men and guns. The gunners, with an escort of seventy militia, pressed on ahead of the main force and were ambushed just west of the town at Three Rocks. They were shot and piked to death, all but three of them, and the rebels gained the guns. The events were reported in the *London Gazette* rather differently:

> *Dublin Castle, June 2.* Accounts have been received from Major-General Eustace, at New Ross, stating, that, Major-General Fawcett having marched with a company of the Meath Regiment from Duncannon Fort, this small force was surrounded by a very large body between Taghmon and Wexford, and defeated. General Fawcett effected his retreat to Duncannon Fort. The rebels are in possession of Wexford but a large force is marching to dislodge them.

It does not say, presumably because the commander of New Ross had no news of it, that early the next day, Wednesday, Watson led a party out of Wexford expecting to meet Fawcett. At Three Rocks they, too, were attacked but managed to get clear. Watson, however, was struck down by a shot from a fowling-piece. With the loss of their commander the garrison, in a trickle at first and then in a flood, ran away. The rebels poured into the town and helped themselves to whatever they desired. An eye-witness, Charles Jackson, wrote:

> We passed through crowds of rebels, who were in the most disorderly state, without the least appearance of discipline. They had no kind of uniform but were most of them in the dress of labourers, white bands round their hats and green cockades being the only marks by which they were distinguished ... Their arms consisted chiefly of pikes of an enormous length, the handles of many being sixteen or eighteen feet long. Some carried rusty muskets.

Quite why Mr Jackson should seem surprised at their clothes and weapons is hard to see; these men were labourers and the pikes they had were what the yeomanry had been looking for a long time since. He went on to report how the women were shouting their support of the Croppies. The revolutionaries with their French-style cropped hair had arrived. A Protestant of standing who had been imprisoned as a United Irish sympathiser, Bagenal Harvey, was made commander-in-chief of the rebel army and, in Wexford itself, a Committee of Public Safety was set up. The next step was to divide the force into three parts, one to drive north to take Gorey, one to attack the garrison at Newtownbarry, now called Bunclody, and the third, under Harvey, to seize the strategically important town and river crossing at New Ross.

The venture against Newtownbarry was an unhappy one. The *London Gazette* published a communication from Camden – not a disinterested source – dated 2 June.

> ... a dispatch was this day received ... from Col. L'Estrange, of the King's County [Offaly] Militia, which states, that the town of Newtown Barry had been attacked yesterday morning by a very considerable body of rebels from Vinegar Hill [east of Enniscorthy]. They surrounded the town in such a manner that Col. L'Estrange at first retreated, in order to collect his force. He then attacked the rebels; drove them through the town, with great slaughter, and pursued them several miles, until night obliged them to return. Above 500 of the rebels were killed. Col. L'Estange's detachment consisted of 230 of the King's County Militia, 27 Dragoons, and about 100 Yeomen ...

General Lake was taking steps to deal with the rebels. Major-General Loftus was ordered to advance with his 250 men into County Wexford from Wicklow together with reinforcements in the shape of 400 men and three guns from Dublin under the entirely inexperienced Colonel Walpole, Camden's *aide de camp*. Loftus had Lord Ancram's King's County Militia, with Colonel L'Estrange, on his western flank, his own force on the east and, west to east, two companies moving from Carnew and Colonel Walpole's to Loftus's right. Walpole thrust ahead of the line, contrary to the advice of his fellow officers, and at Tubberneering, in a deep, hedge-lined road, his force was ambushed in what was now classic style.

> *Dublin Castle, June 5, 5 p.m.* Major Marley is just arrived from Major General Loftus; and brings an account that the Major-General, finding that Col. Walpole's detachment had received a check, thought it prudent to move to Carnew, which he effected without the loss of a man. It appears that Col. Walpole had met with the main body of the rebels in a strong post near Slievebuy Mountain, and, having attacked them, he was unfortunately killed by a shot in the head in the beginning of the action, when his Corps being in a situation where it could not act with advantage, was forced to retire to Arklow. The loss was fifty-four men killed and missing, and two six-pounders ...

New Ross, seen from the summit of Slieve Coillte, south of the town.

In fact the line of retreat was further to the west, leaving Arklow vulnerable, as the Government was eventually to realise. The rebels now held almost all of Wexford, but had failed to break out into Carlow at Newtownbarry. They might yet smash their way out in the west, at New Ross.

The Norman town of New Ross was probably founded on a Viking site which marked the limit of easy access of their sea-going boats to the upper reaches of the River Barrow. Here the river was bridged, the lowest point that, at the time, it was possible to do so and thus the town commanded the road west from Wexford to Waterford. If Bagenal Harvey's army was to get out of the county only the eastern coast by way of Arklow or this route were available to him. After its surrender to Oliver Cromwell the defences had been destroyed for the most part; the walls stood but the turrets from which fire could be brought to bear on attackers had probably been reduced and the gateways most likely lacked gates. Further, in these days of cannon, the surrounding hills gave excellent opportunity for gunfire to do considerable damage.

The commander in New Ross was Major-General Henry Johnson from Kilternan, County Dublin. He provided for attacks from two directions, the east, near what is now called Bishop's Gate, the Market Gate of the time, and the south east around Three Bullet Gate. Trenches were dug at both points, the one outside the Three Bullet Gate being angled to overlook both the Wexford road and the road going due south. Major Vandeleur with the Clare Militia held the area of Bishop's gate and the newly-arrived Dublin Militia under Lord Mountjoy were at Three Bullet Gate. A strongpoint, the Main Guard, was formed at the junction of Mary Street and South Street with guns that could be aimed along either of the roads. The bridge at the time was a block further north, not, as now, connecting with Mary Street. The cavalry were to form a reserve on the quay. He had, according to some accounts, something like four or five hundred men while Francis Grose says 'near one thousand seven hundred'. Johnson had taken the precaution of disarming the civilian population, allegedly for their own safety, but some accounts speak of civilians shooting in support of the troops. As usual, the truth is elusive.

The rebels, perhaps 8,000 men, left their camp at Three Rocks outside Wexford on 31 May but dawdled on the way and did not reach the outskirts of New Ross until 4 June. Some of the time was spent in rounding up people they did not like and confining them in a barn at Scullabogue. They eventually made their camp on Corbet Hill, south east of the town, having given Johnson plenty of time to prepare himself. At 3.30 a.m. on 5 June Bagenal Harvey summoned General Johnson to surrender the town, sending one Matthew Furlong of Raheen with the message. As he approached the town's outposts Furlong was shot and killed, in spite of his flag of truce or by mistake it is impossible to say. His comrades saw him fall and immediately John Kelly of Killan led 500 Bantrymen into the attack, swarming over the outer defences and threatening Three Bullet Gate. They tried using the cattle-driving tactic that had worked at Enniscorthy, but here the herd was deflected by the angled trench and the fire of the defenders. In the fierce fighting Lord Mountjoy was killed.

General Johnson sent the 5th Dragoons, the Royal Irish Regiment of Dragoons, into action and they rode into the fields outside the gate. The rebels made vigorous use of their pikes and the horsemen suffered severely. Francis Grose's account, published in 1812, recounts:

> This was a service replete with danger, as from the situation of the place, and the continual increase of a desperate enemy, a handful [sixty] of men seemed precluded from every hope of escaping destruction. Notwithstanding, the order was instantly obeyed, and the detachment rode to meet the bodies of insurgents advancing against them, armed with pikes from ten to twelve feet long. Nor were the rebels inexperienced in the practice of this formidable weapon. Their instructions were to pierce the horse in the flank, and thus obtain easy conquest over the rider. In this conflict the heavy squadron was almost entirely cut to pieces, or disabled. The quarter-master of the fifth dragoons, on whom the command at last devolved, accompanied by only nine men, with difficulty made good his retreat ...

The Government forces had to withdraw into the town and the attackers surged after them. Some ran along Neville Street towards St Mary's Church, but a gun in the churchyard opened fire on them. Another gun fired along Chapel Lane on men in Mary Street. John Kelly led his men down Michael Street as far as the barracks, where he fell wounded. Others reached the riverside. The southern half of the town

New Ross, looking along part of Bewley Street, called Neville Street at that time, to Church Lane and St Mary's. From the churchyard a cannon hurled grapeshot along the narrow street into the attacking insurgents, inflicting terrible casualties.

was in rebel hands and much of it was now on fire. The Main Guard and the Bishop's Gate positions were still firmly in government hands and General Johnson rallied his remaining men who had retreated over the bridge.

While some of the attackers started to seek food and drink, others prepared to launch an attack along the narrow street running from the barracks on Michael Street to its junction with Mary Street east of the Main Guard. Up this street, variously called Michael's Lane, Barrack Lane or Bakehouse Lane, a murderous musket fire was maintained, cutting the pikemen down and forcing them to fall back. Johnson now led his men back over the river and began to clean street after street with cannon-fire. The action swung back and forth, to and from Three Bullet Gate, as the afternoon wore on. Rebels in the houses burned to death or were shot as the soldiers found them. A last, futile, effort was made to attack through Irishtown, near Bishop's Gate, but it was too feeble and too late. As the day drew to a close, the medical officer later wrote, 'The remaining part of the evening was spent in searching for and shooting the insurgents, whose loss in killed was estimated at two thousand, eight hundred and six men.'

The return of killed, wounded and missing made by General Johnson was as follows:

The quayside, New Ross. The modern bridge connects with Quay Street and Mary Street, but the bridge of the time, over which Johnson led his troops, was to the left.

The narrow coastal plain at Wicklow, showing the easternmost line of advance of the insurgents.

Killed: 1 Colonel, 1 Cornet, 1 Quarter Master, 4 Sergeants, 3 Drummers, and 81 rank and file; also 54 horses; wounded, 1 Captain, and 57 rank and file, also 5 horses; missing, 1 Captain, 3 Lieutenants, 1 Ensign, 2 Sergeants, 2 Drummers, 72 rank and file, and 4 horses.

With their failure at New Ross only one route out of the south east remained to the rebels, the coast road which crossed the River Avoca at Arklow.

The total number killed in the New Ross sector of operations was rather larger. In the town the troops, once their adversaries had been ejected, ran amok. It was hours before they were brought under control, and during that time the innocent suffered as much as those who had been in arms against them. Houses were ransacked, food, drink and valuables taken and the view of the regular soldiers, that the Government forces within Ireland were possibly more dangerous than the rebels, was validated. On the insurgent side there were terrible doings as well. In the confusion of partial news coming to the rear about the storming of New Ross an alleged order was received to execute the captives at Scullabogue. The local commander refused at first, but in the face of repeated messages he eventually went ahead. The unfortunate men were, at first, forced to kneel in rows of four at a time and shot. Another group were busy stopping up the barn in which the families had been confined. Thirty-five men were shot, but when the barn was set ablaze more than a hundred men, women and children perished in the flames.

After the Gorey Races, as the British army later called the action at Tubberneering, about six hundred of Colonel Walpole's defeated force sped their way past Gorey and back to Arklow, where Captain Rowan was positioned with seventy-eight men of the Antrim Militia. Sir Watkin Williams Wynne, now in command of the fugitives, had gathered up everyone and made for Wicklow town. On 5 June General Francis Needham was given the task of setting matters in better order and preventing the United Irish forces coming north. Together with six hundred men of the Cavan Militia under Colonel Maxwell he reached Wicklow and proceeded next day to Arklow with the rest of the available force, totalling now about a thousand. Small groups of the 5th and 9th Dragoons joined on 7 June and General Lake supplied 300 Loyal Durham Fencibles and 128 Dumbarton Fencibles, both infantry units. These last arrived on 9 June, the day of the fight. Meanwhile the insurgents had been frittering away their opportunities in foraging for food and a punitive expedition on Carnew. For a second time the inability to exploit the Government weakness was to lose them their objective.

In 1798 Arklow stood on the south side of the river and consisted of one main street with the barracks at the western end, where traces of it can still be found. The bridge to the north was at the other, eastern, end and survives now. A road, now no more than a path, ran by the sea from the two hills, Arklow Rock and Little Rock, to the part of town south of the bridge, the Fishery. Another road, the Coolgreany Road, came from the west and the Yellow Lane connected them. The modern road from Gorey and the railway did not exist at the time. Two tributaries to the Avoca flow

The bridge at Arklow. The town at the time ran mainly to the right and a few hovels stood to the left.

from the south west; one in a ravine past the barracks (near the railway station) and the other across the Arklow Rock road east of the bridge. As a defensive position it leaves much to be desired, except for the field of fire it commands. On the west Needham had three 6-pounder guns, one probably on a platform in the barrack yard and the other two close to a barricade blocking the Coolgreany Road just east of the stream. Here he positioned about 550 men as well. The east end of the town was defended by a barricade south of the bridge and east of the old churchyard and two guns. In between there was a thin line of men to hold the south of the position.

At about 10 a.m. on 9 June the rebels moved out of Gorey. There were some 20,000 of them, armed with pikes, some muskets and agricultural tools and a couple of captured cannon. It took more than six hours to reach Arklow, where they encountered outposts with which they exchanged fire but, when they gathered to charge them, the defenders made off back to the main defensive positions and gave the alarm. Some of the United forces turned off along the Yellow Lane towards the Fishery while others came on along the Coolgreany Road with one of the guns. Another gun was taken along the Yellow Lane and was sited at extreme range, south of the town. The Dumbarton Fencibles were in the ditches and hedges west of the town and after exchanging shots with the rebels rushed back to the barricade. Encouraged by the appearance of success, the attackers charged towards the barricade, only to be met by the power of two 6-pounders firing grape shot. The mass of insurgents staggered back into the fresh men coming up and the force began to filter off to the right, along the southern flank held by the Durhams. Here, in the natural cover of hedges and ditches, impromptu trench warfare started with both sides sniping as best they could. Attempts were made to charge the town, but across the open ground between the forces it was suicide. The combination of musket fire from three ranks of infantry and grapeshot from the cannon prevented any rebels reaching Needham's lines for hand-to-hand fighting.

In the east the rebels managed to get behind the outposts on the Arklow Rock Road and set fire to the pitiful huts of the poorest part of town, the Fishery. Sir Watkin Wynne brought his cavalry over the bridge and attempted to break up the rebels but, as at New Ross, his men were badly mauled by pikemen undaunted by sword-wielding dragoons. General Needham wrote in his report that they '... charged the rebels most gallantly, and routed a strong column of them attempting to gain the town ...' This does not sit credibly with the fact that the fighting on this flank was hard and long, the explanation for which is that the barricade was most effective. The guns hurled their grapeshot amongst the attackers with devastating results. Men rushed forward to fill the great gaps smashed in their formations and charged again, and again the cannon cut them down.

On the west the rebel cannon was worked at first by men constrained to serve through threat of violence, but later the rebels themselves took over and had some success; some later said too much success as the pikemen tended to stand about and admire their shooting instead of engaging Needham's troops. Captain Fleming of the Royal Irish Artillery took exception to his adversary's good aim in destroying a gun carriage, ordered roundshot to be loaded and engaged Edmond Kyan's piece, knocking off Kyan's artificial arm and wounding him seriously enough for him to be taken out of action.

At about 8 p.m. both sides were getting low on ammunition, not that their enemies knew it, and with affairs still in the balance Father Michael Murphy of Ballycanew turned up. As he came along the Coolgreany Road he met men coming away and turned them back. He rallied the pikemen for another charge and led it himself. The nearer they got to the western barricade the more men fell to musket fire. Then the guns spoke. The priest was caught in a hail of canister shot and fell dead. The pikemen pulled back behind their musketeers and the musketeers began to turn away; they had no more ammunition. On the other flank the rebels also started to pull out, the last of them encouraged to leave by Maxwell's Cavan Militia setting fire to the hovels they had used for cover. The Dragoons had a final gallop to clear the field. At 8.30 p.m. the action ceased, but, uncertain about the morrow, the Government forces held their ground. Major Hardy, the commander at Wicklow, had been apprised of the ammunition shortage and hurried further supplies to General Needham against a renewal of the fight, but it was not, in the event, needed. The United Irish had gone back to Vinegar Hill, outside Enniscorthy.

As a defensive position Vinegar Hill is unremarkable. It has all the problems associated with the motte; it is hard to supply with food and water, it is easily surrounded and any attempt to make a sally from it is easily observed and countered. Further, in an age of artillery, it can form something disturbingly close to a shooting gallery with the defenders as the targets. The United Irish retired to this vulnerable place and waited there for ten days, doing nothing to provide for their future fight. Meanwhile reinforcements were arriving in Ireland and soon General Lake was able to assemble a force of 10,000 men to regain Wexford and leave a similar number to deal with matters elsewhere. What was more important was the artillery he had: twenty guns. Lake moved against the rebels with four columns. Lake reported to Lord Cornwallis, who had just been appointed lord lieutenant and commander-in-chief, on 21 June:

> ... the rebel camp upon Vinegar-hill was attacked this morning, at 7 o'clock, and carried in about an hour and a half. The relative importance of this very strong position with our operations against Wexford made it necessary to combine our attacks so as to ensure success. A column, under Major-Generals Johnson and Eustace, was drawn from Ross, and began the attack upon the town of Enniscorthy, situate upon the right [west] bank of the Slaney, close

The inhospitable summit of Vinegar Hill.

under Vinegar-hill, upon the right, and rather to the rear of it. Lieut.-Gen. Dundas commanded the centre column; two other columns were commanded by Major-Generals Sir James Duff and Loftus and a fourth column on the left, by the Hon. Major-Gen. Needham. To the determined spirit with which these columns were conducted, and the great gallantry of the troops, we are indebted to the short resistance of the rebels, who maintained their ground obstinately for the time above mentioned; but on perceiving the danger of being surrounded, they flew with great precipitation ... great praise is due to the Earl of Ancram and Lord Roden, for their gallant charge with their regiments at the moment the cavalry was wanted to complete the success of the day ... To the rapid and well-directed fire of the Royal Artillery ... I consider myself this day highly indebted ...

It was, in fact, the artillery that did the greatest damage to the insurgents on the hill. They withstood the bombardment for about an hour and then the cavalry charged from Lake's side, the east. In spite of the fulsome praise in the report, Needham took little part in the action. His men, already tired by a full day's pitched battle, unlike the British newcomers, had lagged behind, dallying with the slaughter of any unfortunates they cared to deem as rebels on their way from Arklow. As a result, when the rebels eventually broke and fled off the hill, their way south was open and many escaped. Those remaining, including a large number of women and children, were put to the sword. In Enniscorthy itself a fierce fight had taken place.

The victory revealed the strength of the artillery acquired by the United Irish and it was, no doubt, a cause for thanksgiving that they lacked the skilled men to make use of it.

> *Return of ordnance, and c. taken from the rebels on Vinegar-hill, June 21.* 2 brass 6-pounders, side-arms complete; 1 brass ditto, ditto; 1 metal 6-pounder, no drag-ropes; 6 metal 1-pounders, ditto; 1 metal 3-pounder; 1 brass 5 1/2-inch howitzer; 1 brass 4 1/2-inch ditto. 13 total.

In Wexford the 'Republic' had been dealing with the threat of mob rule which reached a climax in the execution of prisoners at the instigation of one Captain Thomas Dixon, who organised a so-called court to try them. Ninety-seven died before a Catholic priest intervened to stop the wanton slaying. Fortunately General Lake did not hurry to the town's relief, for his interest in withholding his men from committing atrocities appears to have been minimal. From the west came Sir John Moore at the head of 2,000 men. The rebels delayed him a little at Foulkmills but the next day he met emissaries from the town and appreciated that the prisoners would suffer if he failed to accept a negotiated surrender. He was heavily outnumbered and, on 21 June, made a cautious approach, at which his adversaries fled. There were more skirmishes in the south east before the uprising was finally over, but the main danger to British rule was now past. What followed horrified Cornwallis. Brutality, murder, plunder and other horrors were inflicted on the populace and only with difficulty brought under control.

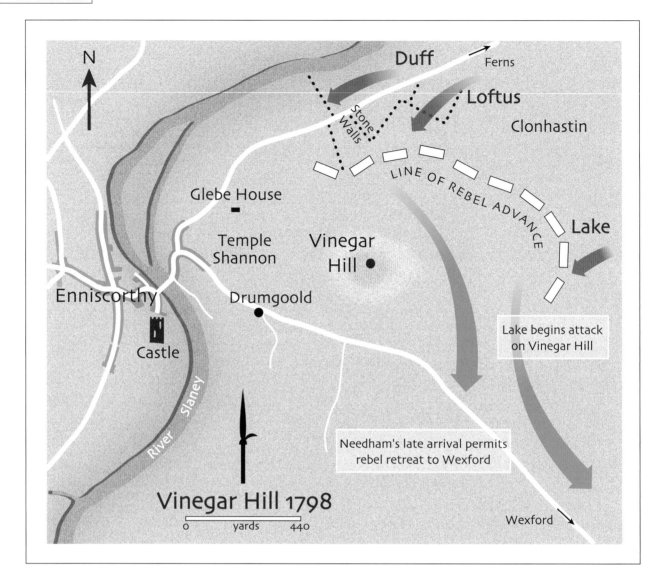

N

Duff

Ferns

Loftus

Stone Walls

Clonhastin

Glebe House

LINE OF REBEL ADVANCE

Temple
Shannon

Vinegar
Hill

Lake

Enniscorthy

Drumgoold

Lake begins attack
on Vinegar Hill

Castle

River Slaney

Needham's late arrival permits
rebel retreat to Wexford

Vinegar Hill 1798

0   yards   440

Wexford

The remnants of the rebels found sanctuary in the Wicklow Mountains. Michael Dwyer and his band remained a threat and in February 1800 the 'principal magistrates and gentlemen of the county of Wicklow' petitioned Cornwallis to have roads constructed to facilitate the swift passage of troops to combat them. With the fear of a French invasion encouraging action, the road was built. It started at Rathfarnham, south of Dublin, and ran due south to Glencree where there was a barrack, and on to the Sally Gap, leaving Lough Tay and Lough Dan to the east as it made its way to Laragh. The barrack here survives in part as a residence, and the bastions at two corners of the perimeter wall can be seen. The road then runs to Drumgoff in Glenmalure where the ruins of the barrack, three storeys high, still guard the way. The road ended some way to the south west at Aughavannagh where, in the 1990s at least, the barrack was a youth hostel. What was constructed as a tool for military domination has become a journey through a peaceful and outstandingly beautiful landscape.

The Military Road climbing north out of Glenmalure. It was completed late in 1809 at a cost of some £70,000.

Drumgoff Barracks, Glenmalure. In addition to the main barrack building the perimeter wall, gateway and two corner bastions survive. Each of the five barracks on the road was intended to have a garrison of a captain and 100 men, except for Leitrim which had twice as many men.

3

The Narrow Doors of Munster

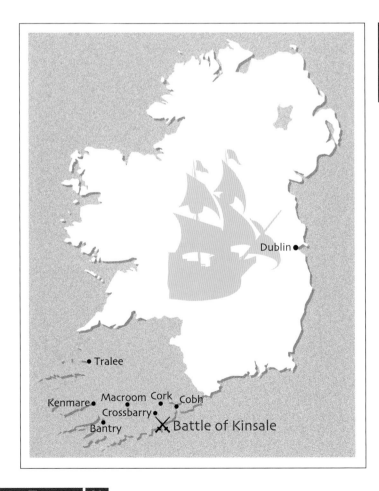

East of a line from north to south through Limerick and Cork the country is relatively easy of passage, but west of that line it has the look of lofty land savagely attacked with a rake. The great lines of hills and mountains run to the south west to lose themselves in the waters of the Atlantic from which their final eminences, the Skellig and Fastnet Rocks, rear their heads before the grey waters close in. The constraints of the western country favour small, mobile groups of warriors rather than grand armies while the generous harbours of Cork and Kinsale invite the invader to enter the central heart of Ireland.

Looking north from the Healy Pass in the Caha Mountains, north of Bantry Bay, towards Kilmakillogue Harbour on the southern shore of the Kenmare River; difficult country for large military formations.

Staigue Fort, built in drystone, gave refuge some 2,000 years ago in circumstances at which one can only guess.

The first invaders in recorded history, the Vikings, were sea-rovers to whom the physical challenges of dry land were irrelevant. They came from both directions. From the north the raids reached Sligo in A.D. 807 and four years later they raided the lonely monastic outposts on the Skelligs. Eleven years after that, in 822, the raiders of Ireland's east coast had progressed along the southern shore as far as Cork and in 827 they came into Kinsale harbour. Next they attempted to settle at Rosscarbery and no doubt they entered Bantry Bay but if they stayed at all they did not stay long. Their efforts were resisted and it was only at Cork and Limerick that Viking towns were established.

A Trace of Normans

The Norman influence in the east of the country is substantial, but, as the source of that was the Norman kingdom in England, the farther away one was the better one's chance of escaping their attentions. Nonetheless they penetrated well into this country in spite of Diarmaid MacCarthaigh of Cork's ploy of swearing fealty to Henry II in 1171 to secure his own hold on the territory. That the attempt to exclude the Normans was a failure is shown by the fact that in 1185 they had advanced as far as Durrus, south west of Bantry, but from there they were pushed back to the east. Numerous fortifications were built and subsequently sacked. It is said that the Carew family built a castle at Dún na mBarc, now Donemark, although the work has also been attributed to the MacCarthaighs. It was, in any case, entirely destroyed by Finghin MacCarthaigh in 1260.

The isolated Skelligs. The seventh-century monastery founded by St Finian on Skellig Michael, in the distance, was raided by Vikings.

Finghin was not in conflict solely with the Normans, but also with Irish chiefs allied to them. The Geraldine leader of the time, John FitzThomas FitzGerald, had become Finghin's overlord by acquiring Desmond in 1259 and also supported the kingship of his supposed vassal's cousin, Domhnall Ruadh MacCarthaigh. The consequential destruction of FitzThomas's castles and those of his fellow Munster colonists and the raiding of their lands provoked a punitive expedition. In August 1261 the combined Norman and Irish army marched into the narrow valleys and over the high passes in search of their quarry and Finghin MacCarthaigh was careful to select a battleground suited to his own, lightly armed and nimble fighters.

The deep inlet north of Bantry Bay, the Kenmare River, narrows to the north east at the town of Kenmare where it is fed by a river running down from Kilgarvan. From Kilgarvan a road goes south, next to a small tributary of the Kenmare, over the pass in the Shehy Mountains and down to Bantry. Finghin chose to fight where this little river, the Ruachtach, forks and is joined by the Slaney hurrying down from the pass, and the valley narrows abruptly. The place is called Callan. The terrain is wooded and the going rough. Finghin brought his enemies to battle in the fork of the streams and surrounded them. John FitzThomas FitzGerald and his son Maurice were killed together with the son of Walter de Burgo, fifteen knights and more than three hundred men. The defeat of the Geraldines allowed the victorious Finghin MacCarthaigh to set out on a rampage of destruction that took him to the very

The snaking line of trees marks the course of the Slaney River running down to the site of the Battle of Callan in the distance.

outskirts of Kinsale where he beseiged the de Courcy castle of Ringrone, the thin, surviving towers of which still stand on the southern bank of the River Bandon, across the water from the town. Here, at Bearnach Reanna Roin, Finghin was attacked by Miles de Cogan at night. The slaughter of the Irish was comprehensive. Domhnall Ruadh MacCarthaigh was the beneficiary as Maurice FitzGerald's son, Thomas, was new-born and the Earl of Desmond was thus unable to challenge his Irish vassal for close on twenty-one years, by which time the MacCarthaigh hold on the south west, bounded by Kinsale in the south and Tralee in the north, was unshakeable.

The Spanish Threat

The MacCarthaigh, or McCarthys as they became, and the FitzGeralds of Desmond held this country without much change in their territories well into Tudor times. As long as all remained quiet, English attention was on other things which would, in the fullness of time, have a grave impact on Ireland. With the end of the Wars of the Roses and the arrival of Tudor monarchs, things changed and the ancient Irish, or rather, Celtic institutions, Brehon laws and traditional customs were destined to disappear. The increasing centralisation of government brought changes in the east at first, but when that was coupled with the Reformation the polarisation of the populace into Protestant rulers and Catholic subjects began, precipitated by the rising led by Silken Thomas, Lord Offaly, the son of the Earl of Kildare, in 1534 and the subsequent legislation. What was worse was the impact of external enmities, the continental Wars of Religion and the threat of Spanish intervention with the succession of Elizabeth I to the throne.

In addition to the usual cattle raiding and inter-chieftain rivalries that go largely unremarked there were more serious uprisings. James FitzMaurice FitzGerald, the most influential of the Geraldines and a robust Catholic, sought the support both of the Pope and of Spain when he rebelled in 1569. FitzMaurice had 1,400 gallowglass, mercenaries of foreign, usually Scottish, origin who fought with axes, 400 pikemen, 400 musketeers and 1,500 kerne (lightly-armed Irish mercenaries). The castle of Tracton, west of Cork, was stormed in June, the garrison killed and the country round about laid waste. Black Tom Butler, tenth Earl of Ormond, undertook the task of

In the tight, wooded country through which the Slaney runs the Normans were unable to exploit their cavalry.

A spear-carrying gallowglass with conical helmet – a tomb carving from Dungiven Priory, County Derry.

subduing the rising and a series of small skirmishes and sieges took place. Colonel Humphrey Gilbert bested James FitzMaurice FitzGerald near Cork and then took his twenty-three castles one by one, slaughtering everyone in them if they failed to yield promptly. The fighting trailed on with FitzMaurice supplementing his forces as needful with 'naughty idle' MacSweeney and MacSheehy gallowglass. When, rarely, the rebel could be brought to battle the government forces would prevail. When, as was more usual, the mighty royalist column ploughed across the countryside looking for him, the Irish easily out-manouevred it. It was not until November 1572 that FitzMaurice was finally defeated near Kilkenny by Sir Edmund Butler.

Three years later FitzMaurice went to the continent to raise forces for another attempt and landed in the Dingle peninsula in 1579 to begin again. The Spaniards landed in the Dingle peninsula, at Smerwick, in the autumn of 1580, though the force actually had a majority of Italians among its 600 men. They established themselves at Dún an Óir on the western side of the harbour. Lord Grey de Wilton led the force to oppose them, bringing with him eight culverins with which to bombard their positions. They soon surrendered and, apparently contrary to the accepted rules of war, the prisoners were slaughtered. In 1582, the rising still in being under the leadership of Sir John of Desmond, Ormond was appointed Governor of Munster and by the following February Desmond had been driven into the mountains of Kerry. By the autumn he was reduced to a few followers and was finally killed by one of the Moriartys revenging himself for a cattle raid in November 1583. In the aftermath of the rebellion Elizabethan policy was to secure Munster by plantation, that is, by allocating lands to reliable and usually Protestant Englishmen. Some 4,000 people had been brought in by the mid-1590s. In this sorry tale three different policies had been tried by the English: wholesale destruction and laying waste of the land and castles, major forays from fixed garrisons with heavy military forces and, finally, plantation. None was successful. Edmund Spenser, author of *The Faerie Queene*, had come to Ireland in about 1580 and wrote *A View of the Present State of Ireland*, a dialogue between advocates of hard and soft policies which ran into censorship problems in the 1590s. Quite what his own view was is difficult to establish, and his enjoyment of the riches of his Irish estate did not endure, for he died in poverty, landless, in London in 1599. However, his remarks on the problems posed to the English by the Irishman are revealing:

> It is well known that he is a flying enemy, hiding himself in woods and bogs from whence he will not draw forth [save] into some straight passage and perilous ford, where he knows the army must needs pass, there will he lie in wait, and, if he find advantage fit, will dangerously hazard the troubled soldier. Therefore, to seek him out that still flitteth and follow him that can hardly be found would be vain and bootless; but I would divide my men in garrison upon his country in such places as I think must most annoy him.

The impact of the Spanish Armada in 1588 on Munster was minimal, limited to the odd shipwreck, but the effect on the minds of the English was immense. Fear of Catholicism and of the Spanish became ineradicable. The end of the Desmond war

The entrance to Kinsale Harbour. On the left is Charles Fort which assumed the former function of Ringcurran Castle on that flank in guarding the waterway. In the centre is Castle Park with, to the right, James Fort and, on the left, at water level, a blockhouse capable of subjecting shipping to point-blank fire. James Fort, the last creation of Paul Ive, was finished in 1604 and Charles Fort was begun in 1678.

had not brought peace, for Hugh O'Neill, who became Earl of Tyrone in 1593, in attempting to increase his domination of Ulster, claimed for himself the leadership of the Catholic Counter-Reformation. He was declared a traitor in 1595 and conducted a successful war against Elizabeth I's forces in the north of Ireland. The nature of his fight, as seen through English eyes, was defined by the Queen's Irish Council in 1597:

> The rebels stand not as heretofore upon terms of oppression and country grievances, but pretend to recover their ancient land and territories out of the Englishmen's hands, and for the restoring of the Romish religion, and to cast off English laws and government, and to bring the realm to the tanist law [Gaelic elective law of succession], acknowledging Tyrone to be lieutenant to the Pope and the King of Spain.

In 1601 the Spanish intervened in force. Charles Blount, Lord Mountjoy, had been appointed Lord Deputy in 1600 and his growing success against Hugh O'Neill led the Irishman to send a messenger to the Spanish court in June 1601, asking for 6,000 men to turn the tide. The problem was where to send them. The Spanish representative to O'Neill in the previous year, Archbishop Matthew de Oviedo, held that Munster was the place and Kinsale was chosen. A message from Ulster proposing

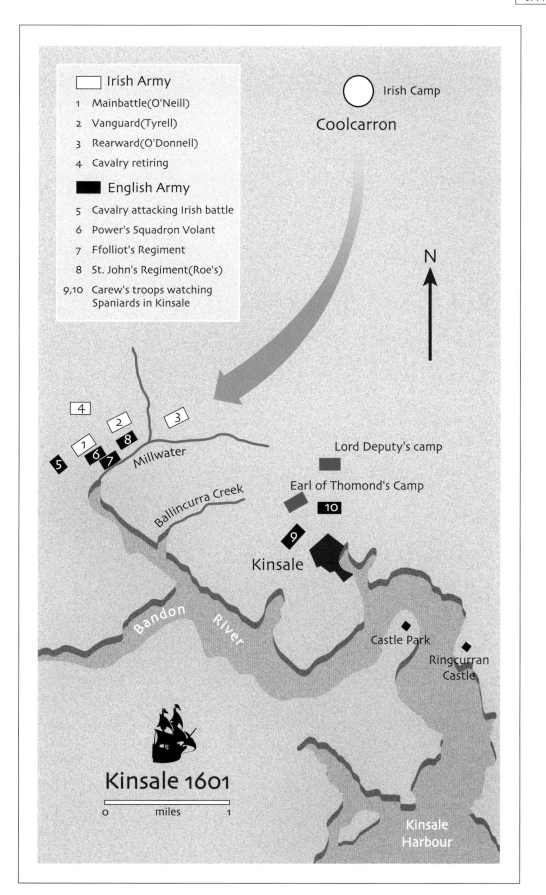

Irish Army

1 Mainbattle(O'Neill)
2 Vanguard(Tyrell)
3 Rearward(O'Donnell)
4 Cavalry retiring

English Army

5 Cavalry attacking Irish battle
6 Power's Squadron Volant
7 Ffolliot's Regiment
8 St. John's Regiment(Roe's)
9,10 Carew's troops watching
       Spaniards in Kinsale

Coolcarron

Irish Camp

N

Millwater

Ballincurra Creek

Lord Deputy's camp

Earl of Thomond's Camp

Kinsale

Bandon River

Castle Park

Ringcurran Castle

Kinsale 1601

0   miles   1

Kinsale Harbour

Limerick or Galway arrived too late; the fleet had sailed thirty-five vessels strong. On 22 September 1601, after encountering a storm, the remaining twenty-six ships carrying 3,500 soldiers entered Kinsale harbour and Don Juan del Aguila entered the town. They established themselves outside the town as well, occupying Ringcurran and Ringrone castles and Castle Park and placed an observation post on Compass Hill. These sites can be identified today. Ringcurran, on the eastern side of Kinsale Harbour, was replaced by Charles Fort, and James Fort was built on the opposite side, at Castle Park. Ringrone Castle is on the southern shore of the Bandon, west of the modern bridge south of Kinsale, and Compass Hill is on the northern side of the river, immediately south of the town.

The reaction of Lord Mountjoy was immediate. He received the news the next day and arrived in Cork on 27 September. Men were summoned from garrisons far away and by 14 October he had 6,900 men in Cork. On 26 October Mountjoy had camped on a hill north east of the town. Fynes Moryson was Lord Mountjoy's private secretary and he wrote an account of his experiences.

> The 17 [October] the army rose, and marching towards Kinsale, encamped within half a mile of the towne under a hill called Knock Robin, where some few shot the Spaniards offered to disturbe our sitting downe ...

> Now the Spaniards held the castle of Rincorane [Ringcurran] from their first landing, and because it commanded the Harbour of Kinsale, so that our shipping could not safely land our provisions neere the Campe, it was thought fit to make the taking thereof our first worke. To which purpose Sir John Barkeley, Sir William Godolphin, and Captaine Josias Bodley Trench-Master were sent to chuse a fit place to plant our Artillerie against the Castle. The twenty-eight day two Colverings [culverins] which had not long been used, were made fit, and the next day they were mounted.

That night the Spanish made a sally by water but were repulsed by Captain Button's ship. The English guns began firing on 30 October, but by evening one of them had broken. The defenders then pulled a cannon out of the town and opened fire on the English camp, smashing a barrel of money in the Paymaster's tent and two barrels of Mountjoy's beer. The next day two more guns were brought to bear on the castle and the bombardment went on all day, in spite of a determined attack by 500 Spanish troops which was, at a cost, thrown back.

> All this while our three pieces battered the Castle, till six of the clock at night, when those of the Castle did beat a Drumme, which the Lord President ... admitted to come unto him. With the Drum came an Irish man borne at Corke, and these in the name of the rest, prayed that with their Armes, Bagge and Baggage, they might depart to Kinsale.

This was refused as the parley, the English insisted, could only be with the castle's commander. Bartholomeo del Clarizo then came, with his leg broken, and demanded

Kinsale inner harbour from the east.

to be allowed to go on the same terms. This was refused and he was summoned to surrender, which he declined, so he was returned to the castle and the bombardment resumed. Eventually, the next day, the garrison had become so keen to give up that they threatened to throw Bartholomeo out of the place and he at last agreed to yield.

> The Spanish thus yeelded, were in number fourescore and sixe, and foure women (whose names I have, but omit them for brevitie), besides a great multitude of Irish Churles, Women and Children, but not any Swordmen; for those skilfull in the wais, had all escaped ...

Ringcurran was back in English hands, but not without a struggle. Castle Park was retaken by the end of November, securing the harbour against reinforcements to the Spanish.

Meanwhile the Irish armies of Hugh O'Neill and Red Hugh O'Donnell were in action in the north. O'Neill tried to tempt Mountjoy away by raiding into County Meath, but the Lord Deputy was not to be distracted from his prime task. O'Donnell was in the process of attacking his cousin in Donegal Abbey. In spite of having to traverse the length of the island and leave their home territories undefended, both commanders determined to head south to the relief of their allies in Kinsale. By the end of October O'Neill had assembled 1,500 foot and 200 horse at Lough Ramor in Cavan and on 9 November, with further reinforcements, he started south. O'Donnell gathered his men at Ballymote in County Sligo and set off on 2 November. Gathering men as they went, they camped near Roscrea with close on 2,000 foot and 300 horse.

Hugh O'Neill was still away to the north, making what seems to have been a fairly leisurely progress, but from the south Red Hugh O'Donnell had word of the approach of Sir George Carew, President of Munster, whom Mountjoy had sent on 7 November towards Cashel with 2,500 men to oppose the relief. O'Donnell led his men away to the west, over the Slievefelim mountains in the snow and ice and down towards Kinsale to approach it from the west. O'Neill was forced to follow a similar route and the two met west of the town of Bandon, north west of Kinsale. Carew meanwhile had returned to Mountjoy's army, unable to keep pace with the Irish.

Aguila had not been idle during this time. On 10 November his men made a sally to attack the English. On 1 December the English cannon made a breach in the town walls and an attempt was made to storm it, but the Spaniards beat it back. On 2 December a Spanish reply was made by making a feint towards the battery to the west of the town before hurling the main attack at the one to the east where the guns were spiked. Later the same night they renewed the push to the west and spiked those guns also. Both armies were suffering from want of food by now. The English had laid waste the country for miles around and the Spaniards could get no supplies by sea. The discomforts of winter also prompted disease and some forty men a day were being lost by Mountjoy as a result. O'Neill wanted to take advantage of the fact by besieging the besiegers and starving the English into surrender, but the Spanish were eager to end their discomfort and O'Donnell was burning to get to blows.

The Irish camped at Coolcarron, just three miles north of Kinsale, on 21 December. They had been reinforced by about 500 Munstermen and by 200 or so Spaniards who had landed at Castlehaven. The English were mainly east and west of the town and close by it. Moryson recorded another English problem: desertion.

> Notwithstanding the severe courses we have taken, by executing some for a terror to the rest ... yet they steale away daily in such numbers, as besides those that by devises doe get passages, there are at present taken betweene this and Waterford, at the least two hundred ready to be returned; though we confesse the misery they indure is such, as justly deserveth some compassion, for divers times some are found dead, standing centinell, or being upon their guard, that when they went thither were very well and lusty, so grievous is a Winters siege, in such a Countrey ...

In the early hours of 24 December, by the old calendar, the Irish moved, apparently on an encircling route to the west, either with a view to joining with a Spanish sally to roll up the English from the south or to reinforce the town, though what advantage putting more hungry mouths into Kinsale would bring is hard to see. Captain Richard Tyrrell led the vanguard of Meath and Leinstermen, Munstermen and the few Spanish. Hugh O'Neill commanded the main battle, composed of Ulstermen, and Red Hugh O'Donnell brought up the rear with men of Tirconnell and Connacht. They made slow progress, groping their way in the pitch darkness, and dawn discovered them well short of their objective. The English discovered them, too. An attack of some kind was expected and Mountjoy may even have been warned. He had, in any case, kept Sir Henry Power's regiment available for three days, relieved of all other duties, to form a *squadron volant*, a flying squad, to be thrown into action whenever and wherever needed. Out in front, or to the rear if viewed from Kinsale town, of English lines was Sir Richard Graeme's force of scouts. The alarm was given in good time.

Mountjoy's standing orders for such an emergency were that five regiments of infantry were to stay in his camp, north east of the town, and four in the Earl of Thomond's camp to the north west of it and three troops of horse were to remain as well. Carew was in command of these forces to keep an eye on the Spaniards in Kinsale and to await developments lest they be needed as a reserve. Mountjoy was to take three infantry regiments, Power's, Ffolliot's and St John's, and most of the cavalry, about 450 horse, giving him about 2,000 men to Carew's 5,000.

The River Bandon runs past Kinsale from a bend west of the town and from that bend Whitecastle Creek reaches back to the north west with two streams entering it. At its apex, farthest from Kinsale, the Millwater creek comes down from the north east and halfway along it the Ballincurra Creek enters on a parallel course. Thus two little valleys lie north west of Kinsale and of Mountjoy's position when he had his first sight

To the right of the road the Millwater stream runs towards the viewer. The O'Neill forces withdrew across it to form up on the hillside on the left.

of Hugh O'Neill's force probably on the far side of the nearest stream. The Irish were still in line of march and Red Hugh O'Donnell had not come up with them, so O'Neill pulled them back over Millwater, Hayes-McCoy has it, and the boggy ground along its banks to the higher ground beyond, his men skirmishing with the English as they went. Mountjoy's Marshal, Sir Richard Wingfield, sent some horse and part of Power's regiment after them and Ffolliot's to follow up. They were held for a while in the boggy valley as Hugh O'Neill's forces formed up in great tercios, blocks of pikemen and musketeers, as was Spanish practice in set-piece battle. Moryson again:

> So the Marshall having the Earl of Clanrickard, and Sir Henrie Davers with him, advanced with some hundred horse, and began with a hundred Harqubusiers ... to give occasion of skirmish on the Bog side, which the rebels with some loose shot entertained, their three Battalions standing firme on the one side of the Bog, and our Fort on the other side.

Wingfield got over the river and his horse attempted a charge, but the body of men bristling with sharp weapons turned the horse aside.

Mountjoy then brought the rest of the horse over. Hayes-McCoy lists Carew's under Sir Henry Danvers and the Earl of Clanrickard's, Graeme's, Fleming's and Taafe's. The Irish light cavalry, unused to the prospect of a formal charge, turned to leave, clashing with their own infantry and disrupting their ranks.

> ... whereupon the Marshal with the horse charged home upon the Reare of the Battaile, and the Irish not used to fight in plaine ground ... were suddenly routed ...

The main battle had formed up as the right wing of the Irish line with the vanguard in the centre and Red Hugh O'Donnell's rearguard coming up to form the left. Power's and Ffolliot's were now advancing against the crumbling main battle and St John's was facing Tyrrell's van. As the main battle broke Tyrrell tried to interpose his force between the advancing English and his faltering comrades and as he did so St John's hit him on the flank. They fell off up the hill where only the Spanish contingent eventually stood as Tyrrell's joined Hugh O'Neill's in flight. O'Donnell's troops never got to grips with their enemies, dissolving into retreat as their commander vainly tried to halt the rout. *The Annals of the Four Masters* recounts:

> O'Donnell advanced to the side of O'Neill's people after they were discomfitted, and proceeded to call out to those who were flying, to stand their ground, and to rouse his own people to battle, until his voice and speech were strained by the vehemence and loudness of the langauge in which he addressed all in general ... But, although they were routed, the number slain was not very great, on account of the fewness of the pursuers, in comparison with those before them.

The English horse did not follow far, exhausted as they were. They fired volleys of guns in celebration, and at this Aguila's men emerged from the town, apparently in expectation of joining the Irish against the English. When they saw only English in

The ruins of Dunboy Castle overlooking Bear Haven.

the field they withdrew with some speed. By noon the English were back in camp. Nine days later the Spanish surrendered and were given safe passage home.

For the Irish the battle was the end. There was much fighting to come, but no realistic chance of stemming the tide of English domination. Donal O'Sullivan Beare had brought, it is said, a thousand followers including the women to the fight at Kinsale, and now he retreated to his castle west of Castletownbere on the western shore of Bantry Bay. The tale we have is very much as told by his nephew, Philip, who was a child at the time and unlikely to be an unbiased chronicler, but a fine tale it is. In 1602 O'Sullivan led a force of his own men and those of various local chieftains against his cousin, Sir Owen, at the castle of Carriganass, near Kealkil, north of Bantry on the Macroom road. It was a punitive foray, Sir Owen having sided with the English, and the raids were extended to other allegedly disloyal people such as the O'Donovans and the MacCarthys. Sir George Carew sent the Earl of Thomond to deal with the breach of the peace.

The government force settled down in various locations around Bantry including Whiddy Island at the head of the bay, and it was on the island that they found themselves attacked by O'Sullivan. The government troops were thrown off the island but O'Sullivan had underestimated their numbers and omitted the naval forces from his calculations, so not much physical harm came to his enemies although they lost their baggage and ammunition. Carew renewed his efforts and brought reinforcements, but the terrain was difficult and attempts to march down the peninsula under the Caha Mountains were easily countered by the Irish. He took to the sea and transported his troops to Bere Island, landing on 5 June. From there, by way of Dinish Island, they made their way to invest Dunboy Castle. The fortification could not stand against artillery and by 18 June much of it was rubble. The last of the garrison blew up what was left as Carew's men stormed it. Fifty-eight surviving defenders were hanged at Castletownbere.

While his people were sacrificing themselves in his cause, Donal O'Sullivan Beare was waiting in the next bay to the north, the Kenmare River, for Spanish help. The ship that arrived brought promises of men rather than real soldiers, money, a bishop and a priest. O'Sullivan used the gold to recruit men to his force, but he was harried by Carew's troops and forced to move north. A march of mythical stature ensued as he made his way to Leitrim. He had about 400 fighting men and another 600 followers at the start and ended with eighteen of the former and seventeen of the latter. Only one woman made it. At one stage, when they had to cross the Shannon River, they were forced to slaughter and skin their horses in order to make curraghs in which to ferry themselves over.

Bantry Bay, The Frenchman's Harbour

When James II lost his throne to William of Orange he fled to France and it was with French help that he made his return to his kingdom. In Ireland the Earl of Tyrconnell had created a largely Catholic army before this crisis and Ireland was the obvious first stepping-stone to regaining what James had lost, for by the end of March 1689 Tyrconnell controlled the whole country with the exception of Enniskillen and Londonderry. French support was less than generous, for the enterprise was seen in Paris as a side-show in the continuing conflict between William of Orange and Louis XIV rather than a fight between William of Orange and James II. A fleet of twenty-two ships delivered James to Kinsale on 12 March together with 7,000 troops and he then journeyed to Dublin, arriving on 24 March.

At this stage it appeared that a complete conquest of Ireland by the Jacobites was inevitable and if that was so the next step would be the invasion of England, perhaps through Scotland. It was time for Louis to raise his bet and he decided to send further troops. A second French fleet was gathered in Brest for the purpose. It consisted of two dozen fighting ships of between forty and sixty guns, three frigates, six fireships and eight transports. The number of troops is usually put at 1,500, although some give it as high as 6,000. The fleet sailed on 5 May and was delayed by a calm and did not reach the Irish coast until noon on 9 May. The wind was north-easterly and attempts to tack up the coast for Kinsale were futile, so Admiral Chateaurenault gave orders to steer south of west towards a sheltered haven in Bantry Bay. Two English men-of-war were sighted, but no contact was made. The next day the French fleet entered Bantry Bay and anchored, leaving the frigates to act as sentinels. The English fleet under Admiral Arthur Herbert was, in effect, a reformed service. James had been Lord High Admiral during the war against the

The Caha Mountains seen across Glengariff Harbour, Bantry Bay.

Dutch and was in that position when the navy won the Battle of Lowestoft in June 1665. When William of Orange became king the navy he found was, in essence, that of his enemy and Herbert, who had been dismissed by James II, was his best choice to command a service about which William must have had his doubts.

Herbert was charged with patrolling off the south coast of Ireland to prevent a French fleet making a passage, but first he had to gather up his own force. It was not until 9 April that he had them collected under his orders in the Scilly Isles and it was 12 April before he was off Cork, gathering intelligence. It appeared that he was already too late as James II was in Dublin and the French had left Kinsale. After gales scattered his vessels, regrouping them, visiting England for fresh orders and getting ships repaired, 27 April saw Herbert at sea again, on the lookout for the French. He sailed down towards Brest and then turned back for Ireland. As they lay off Bantry Bay on 10 May, the watching French frigates sighted the English south of Clear Island, and Herbert's ships in turn saw the French.

On the afternoon of 10 May Chateaurenault decided to land the soldiers and their supplies. The Scottish, Irish and French troops were taken off the larger vessels, together with their arms, ammunition and money, and ferried ashore by the fireships and two of the frigates. Darkness came before they had found a landing place and some were put ashore where the ships anchored east of White Horse Point. They were still there the next day when action commenced.

Dunamore Castle, Clear Island.

The wind was coming from the east, down the bay, and Herbert had difficulty in making progress towards his enemy. Chateaurenault was in no hurry to come to battle and it was 11 o'clock in the morning before he gave the order to attack. By this time Herbert was more than halfway up the bay and the fleets had difficulty because of the narrowness of the seaway. Details of the action are sparse. It seems that personal rivalries amongst the French captains led to their manoeuvring their ships as much to prevent others gaining glory as to engage the English. On the English part, it could be that Herbert brought his fleet into action in a vulnerable state both as to numbers and as to sea-room. Herbert's *Defiance* engaged *Le François* which struck back, doing great damage. More English ships came to help and suffered under the fire of *Le Vermandois* and *Le Duc* while *L'Ardent*, Chateaurenault's ship, took on *Defiance*. After three hours *Defiance* was leaving the bay, severely damaged but leading the attempt to draw the French out into open water. At half past five the French broke off the action.

The next day the landing of the troops was completed and two days passed while they got themselves into good order and arranged their baggage train for the march. The poverty of the place shocked the new arrivals and it was not until they reached Bandon, west of Cork, after two days' march, that they got the first impression of civilisation. On they went to Dublin and thence north to the Boyne. Herbert's efforts to prevent the landings had been in vain and the sea battle had no victor, though each side, naturally, claimed a mighty success.

It was to be more than a century before the bay would see a similar fleet carrying foreign troops. In 1793 Britain went to war with France which was now a revolutionary power. Theobold Wolfe Tone arrived in France in February 1796 and began to conduct a campaign to get the Directory, the French government, to support an uprising led by the United Irishmen. France was an unstable political environment, not only because of rivalries between ambitious politicians, but also because it was alive with spies, some reporting to London. By the time Tone's efforts had led to the formation of an expeditionary force to invade Ireland, the English had a pretty good idea of what was afoot, though not necessarily when it would take place.

The plan formed by the French fell into three distinct parts. First, 5,000 men from the Armée des Côtes de l'Océan were to land in Connacht, taking with them sufficient arms for twice their number. Second, a 6,000-strong force from the same army, and including various people it was considered desirable to have out of France, would follow to Galway Bay. The third element was to come from Holland, 5,000 who would mainly be foreign deserters, and would also go to Galway Bay. The whole was to be under the command of General Lazare Hoche. At the same time an expeditionary force was due to go to India. Whether the confusion, lack of equipment and failure to produce money was the result of deliberate obstruction or mere muddle is hard to say. Admiral Louis Thomas Villaret Joyeuse was not only head of the Indian venture but

Crookhaven, a sheltered anchorage east of Mizen Head.

also in command at Brest where both expeditions were being organised; it does not need much imagination to guess which received the better support. Then Villaret's undertaking was cancelled and Hoche had no competition for the available men. A new admiral was required and the choice fell, curiously, on the sickly, half-blind and uncertain Morard de Galles.

At last, on 15 December, the order was given to sail. On 16 December the Directory changed its mind and sent a cancellation instruction. It arrived too late. The fleet was made up of eighteen ships of the line, thirteen frigates, six corvettes, eight transports, an ammunition ship and various other small vessels making forty-five in all. The men numbered 14,750 souls. Hoche and his chief-of-staff were aboard *Fraternité*, as was Admiral de Galles. The two officers second in command of the navy and the army, Rear-Admiral Bouvet and General de Grouchy, were on *L'Immortalité* and Adjutant-General Smith, alias Wolfe Tone, was on Commodore Jacques Bedout's *L'Indomptable*. In the afternoon of 16 December the fleet made its way out of Brest and, as a result of the confusing orders given by de Galles, got broken up, one ship *Séduisant* being lost with 1,265 men. They had sealed orders to rendezvous off Mizen Head (which is south of Bantry Bay), cruise there for five days and if the fleet had not assembled by then to go to the Shannon estuary and wait there for another three days.

Then there was fog. On 19 December Bouvet's flotilla and the eight ships under Rear-Admiral Joseph Neilly met and a conference aboard *L'Immortalité* was convened. In the absence of their commanders-in-chief who were still far to the south, they decided to proceed either to Bantry Bay or the Shannon and land. There were now thirty-four ships left. The sea was calm on 20 December as they laid a course for Mizen Head, but two days later a gale had scattered them again and the east-south-easterly wind was forcing them towards Dursey Island, west of the entrance to the Bay. Neilly ordered his ships to beat into Bantry Bay and as they struggled to do so fishermen put out to pilot them in and brought news that there were no English ships about and that only a couple of hundred men, local militia, were present to defend the area. The weather worsened and it was not until about 4 o'clock in the afternoon of 23 December that *L'Immortalité* anchored between the eastern end of Bere Island and the southern shore. Another fifteen vessels followed her in. In the evening's darkness Neilly's *Résolue* and *Redoutable* collided off the western end of the island and the former had difficulty in anchoring some way to the south. About twenty vessels had failed to enter the bay.

The arrival of the enemy did not go unremarked. The landlord of a hostelry in Bantry, Richard White, sent a message to Cork which arrived about the same time as the English sloop *Kangaroo* reported her sighting of the French fleet. The neighbourhood was very frightened, as a letter quoted by Michael Carroll attests.

Bearhaven 22 December 1796
To Richard White
My Dr Friend,
The French fleet consisting of twenty-eight ships of the Line and some small

vessels are at this moment off this harbour all beating up for Bantry. What we are to do or what is to become of us God only knows.

I am as Ever, yr

Saml Bayley

On the morning of 24 December a conference was held on board *L'Immortalité*. They decided to land what men and stores they could the next morning and signals were later given to move to the designated anchorage. It is not clear from written records where that was. The standing orders indicated Bear Haven, east of Castletown Bearhaven and south of the shore between Mill Cove and Bank Harbour if the wind was in the east. In the case of westerlies the anchorage was to be at Glengariff Harbour at the north-western corner of the bay and a northerly wind created conditions which made the eastern end of Whiddy Island appropriate. In any case the easterly wind increased to a gale by six o'clock in the evening and the weather became worse as Christmas Day dawned and continued bad all day. At half past four in the afternoon Rear-Admiral Bouvet's inclination to get out to sea was increased by the parting of *L'Immortalité's* starboard anchor cable. Her port anchor began to drag and the danger of being driven aground on Bear Island was very real. The port anchor cable was cut and she made for the open sea, signalling others to follow. When, three days later, the weather calmed, she was far to the south-west and, with only one anchor left and uncertain as to the fate of the rest of the fleet, she made for Brest, arriving on 1 January. A longboat from *Résolue* had been sent to help *L'Immortalité* when she was dragging her anchor, but it was blown ashore on Bear Island and its commander, one Lieutenat Proteau, and his men were captured by a troop of yeomanry under Daniel O'Sullivan who took them to Bantry, from where they were sent to Dublin. The longboat is now in the National Museum of Ireland.

In Bantry Bay the gale had blown itself out by 27 December. Wolfe Tone resigned himself to the fact that the expedition could not now continue. A conference was held aboard *L'Indomptable* chaired by General Harty, an Irish officer, the most senior man attending. Tone advocated attempting a landing by way of the Shannon, a scheme already allowed for in their orders. They agreed to go and at four that afternoon the remaining ships, five frigates and lesser vessels and seven ships of the line, left Bantry Bay. Almost immediately a fresh gale struck them and, although *L'Indomptable* reached their destination, she found herself alone. On 29 December she set sail for France.

In Bantry Bay new ships were arriving, the missing French and two other merchant ships, the American *Beaver* and a Guinea trader, the *Sisters*. Many of the vessels had suffered extensively in the storms and their cargos were damaged. Some had been forced to jettison their guns to survive. Although there were now about 4,000 men in the bay they were no longer equipped to undertake military activity. The damaged *Surveillante* was scuttled outside Glengariff harbour, the merchantmen's crews were made to abandon their ships and the vessels were burnt and the French flotilla left the bay. Although further orders were issued and

Wolfe Tone Square, Bantry.

signals exchanged between the remaining ships of the invasion force with the intention of continuing the enterprise, nothing came of them. Eventually the survivors, separated by foul weather and running short of supplies, made their way back to France.

The whole affair confirmed in English minds the danger always present of an invasion of Ireland being a step on the way to an invasion of England. It also affirmed the threat constituted by the United Irishmen and such vigorous steps were taken to arrest the leaders of the movement that the subsequent risings of 1798 lacked coherent direction. On the other side of the coin the presence at all of a French army in Bantry Bay was a considerable propaganda coup which convinced many that the United Irishmen were serious candidates to lead Ireland to independence.

Guns and Signals

Invasion was in everyone's mind as Napoleon's grip on Europe grew. The coastal defences built by Henry VIII were not adequate against modern artillery and the designs of the military engineers sought to go beyond the massive fortifications, such as Fort Charles at Kinsale, that protected a single, key location. After all, the French had just demonstrated their flexibilty and manoeuvrability in bringing an army to Bantry Bay. Further, the British had some excellent information on their enemies' intentions. One Charles François du Périer, General Dumouriez, a French soldier in his sixties, had defected to Britain and, as he had once been in command of the Armée du Nord, had a good deal to tell about the plans his former masters had contrived for invasion. He wrote a report on the Defence of England and also a 'Military Memorandum' on the defence of Ireland. To combat the firepower and mobility of modern navies it was necessary to have good communications and a large number of strongpoints on the coast.

Both the French and the English had been developing signal systems. The French used what became known as semaphore, which took over from an earlier method devised by Claude Chappe and may have derived from using windmill sails arranged in pre-agreed positions. The new semaphore employed three moveable arms on a vertical pole. In England a system of shutters on a frame which made different patterns when open and shut to indicate numbers and letters according to a codebook, Murray's system, was in use in 1796. This was in operation between London and Portsmouth. The coastal signalling system used a combination of balls and flags hoisted on a mast and gaff somewhat similar to the upper masts of a ship. The arrangement of the balls could be changed to convey messages to the next station or, more often, to ships at sea. This system had seventy-four stations on the English coast by 1795 and it was adopted for use in Ireland from 1804. Where it was not associated with a gunnery platform of one kind or another, a signal tower was built – a defensible guard-house, as it was described.

The classic lines of the seventeenth-century Charles Fort overlooking Kinsale Harbour.

From Cork the signal towers spread along the coast, continuing the line of communication from further east. From Carlisle Fort at the entrance to Cork Harbour the line ran to Robert's Head, Barry's Head and thence to Old Head of Kinsale. On they went by way of Seven Heads, Galley Head, Glandore Head, Toe Head, Kedge Point and Cape Clear. Four more towers intervened between Cape Clear and Sheep's Head on the south side of the entrance to Bantry Bay. The next link in the chain was the tower on the western height of Bear Island which communicated with that on Black Ball Head six miles west. Signal station No. 38 on Dursey Island completed the protection of this bay and the line went on towards Valencia Island and beyond to the north.

The new strongpoints took the form of gun batteries, essentially a development of the familiar fort, or of a platform of an entirely new kind, the Martello tower. In 1794 Admiral Samuel Hood took a task force to invade Corsica. Sir David Dundas was in command of the army in this enterprise and recalled the difficulty the gun towers had given them at Cape Mortella when considering the problems of coastal defence in England three years later. Two British warships, the 74-gun *Fortitude* and the 32-gun *Juno*, had been driven off with heavy losses in Corsica. In 1796 a similar tower had been built in South Africa. For the defence of England Dundas suggested:

The signal tower on Dursey Island overlooking the western approaches to Bantry Bay and the Kenmare River.

> ... strong stone towers, favourably situated, not commanded, mounting two or three large guns and protecting as long as proper an outward battery of two more guns, bomb-proof, garrisoned by about thirty men, about 30 feet in height and 12 of interior diameter, entered by a ladder ...

He thought this would be better than building broad, low, conventional batteries at much greater cost. The idea was not taken up for another six years in England and in Ireland it took Robert Emmet's ill-fated Dublin rising in July 1803 to kick-start a programme master-minded by Lieutenant-Colonel Benjamin Fisher. All were agreed that Dublin was the least likely target for an invader, yet that is where the first Martello tower was built in 1804! It may have been the memory of the French in Bantry Bay that led to a tower being built at Glengariff in the same year. The programme as a whole was still under way in 1814.

Four Martello towers were built on Bear Island, of which three remain, but the fortifications surviving also include those of the nineteenth century, and indeed the twentieth, so much has changed. Bearhaven was fortified as a British naval base between 1898 and 1911 and six large gun batteries were constructed. The Whiddy island structures are large circular redoubts, the western one being completed on 18 October 1804. The three defence works were soon finished and eighteen cannon installed. They were manned by seven officers and 188 men and a wooden building

Bearhaven, to the left, was protected by the Martello tower on the skyline, centre, and the batteries at the eastern end of Bear Island.

was put up to meet the problem of overcrowding in the stone structures. It burnt down on 29 December and a few months later the whole garrison was withdrawn from the island. A last flurry of activity took place in 1814 when Garnish Island at the mouth of Glengariff harbour was furnished with a new tower, but that had fallen into disuse just over a decade later.

Land of the Flying Column

In the conflict variously described as the Anglo-Irish War or the War of Independence, the fighting was eventually concentrated in two areas, the country about Dublin and Munster. The British naval presence in Bantry was an obvious target and the local battalion of the Irish Republican Army, as the Irish Volunteers were becoming known at this time, turned their attention from the local Royal Irish Constabulary to a vessel moored at New Pier on 16 November 1919. *Motor Launch 171* was one of 500 built during the First World War. This class of vessel usually had a three-inch anti-aircraft gun or a smaller weapon such as a .303 Vickers-Maxim machine-gun and a crew of nine men. They were just short of ninety feet overall in length, twelve and a half feet in the beam and drew less than four feet of water. *ML 171* has been described as a sloop, but she was a great deal smaller than that.

At seven in the morning the news of *ML 171's* arrival reached the Bantry Volunteers. They had information on the layout of the launch and made plans for a raid. Lookouts were placed and, as it approached ten o'clock that night, eight men cautiously made their way to the railway pier. Maurice Donegan and Ralph Keyes, who were in the lead, saw the sentry go down the companionway and at once jumped on board. The raiders shouted that they had a bomb and the three men on the vessel made no resistance as six rifles and three revolvers were taken from the armoury, together with two black boxes of ammunition. The booty was taken away round the north of the town to the Boys' School. There it was discovered that the ladder they had was too short to allow them into the loft to hide the guns, so they asked the sacristan for permission to conceal the weapons in the loft of the church. Then they made their way to their various homes, undetected. It was typical of numerous small raids for the acquisition of arms.

West of Cork, Commandant General Tom Barry, a former servicemen in the British army, led his famous Flying Column of guerilla fighters in more ambitious missions. The British response to the use of violence was, as one might expect, confused and poorly organised. The Royal Irish Constabulary, which had been declared an agent of an enemy power by the insurgents, was reinforced by a large number of poorly-trained and ill-disciplined men from Britain who could not even be provided with proper uniform. The makeshift garments they wore led to their being named the Black and Tans. In the summer of 1920 yet more men were needed because large numbers of Irish officers of the RIC had been forced by fair means or foul to resign and the Auxiliary Division, Royal Irish Constabulary was set up, a unit under separate command and no better controlled.

The battery at the eastern end of Bear Island.

In August that year a force of 150 Auxiliaries arrived at Macroom, west of Cork, and made themselves prominent within the West Cork IRA Brigade area, the region Tom Barry operated in. On 21 November, at Clogher, north west of Dunmanway, thirty-six men were brought together for training for action against the Macroom-based force. It was known that they often used the road coming south from Macroom to Dunmanway and it was on this road, south of the village of Kilmichael, that it was intended to ambush them. At two o'clock in the morning of Sunday 28 November the Flying Column assembled to have their confessions heard by Father O'Connell of Ballineen before setting off in heavy rain. They marched unseen through the night, pausing for rest and a smoke from time to time. They were some three miles short of their destination when Flyer Nyhan came to Barry and told him that a sixteen-year-old, Pat Deasy, had been following in spite of having been ordered back to Bandon, sick. When questioned about his disobedience he said he was able to go to Bandon by this same route, but hoped his fitness would be recognised and that he would be permitted to join the column. Barry agreed, and the man who had been substituting for him was sent home.

Tom Barry described the place they reached at about a quarter past eight that morning and in which they would fight:

> The point of this road chosen for the attack was one and a half miles south of Kilmichael. Here the north-south road surprisingly turns west-east for 150 yards and then resumes its north-south direction. There were no ditches on either side of the road but a number of scattered rocky eminences of varying sizes. No house was visible except one, 150 yards south of the road at the western entrance to the position.

Barry paraded his men and made the situation clear. Here they were to fight and win; there were no plans for a withdrawal. His exhortations were, according to his own recollection, in an heroic vein and in the cold, damp, grey morning they were, no doubt, needed. The position to be occupied by every man was specified in the hearing of all so that each should know where his comrades were. The commander, Barry, was to take position at the eastern end of the kink in the road, facing the direction from which the Auxiliaries would be coming. There was a small, rough wall, built of loose stone through which one could see and it extended north of the road. With him were three men, Flyer Nyhan, Jim Murphy and Mick O'Herlihy. To the north of the road, about ten paces from the Command Post, there was a large rock, covered with heather. No. 1 Section, ten riflemen, was positioned behind the rock ready to move forward and fire over the top of it when Barry signalled. No. 2 Section, with Michael McCarthy in command, was placed on another rock at the western end of the kink in the road with three men able to bring fire to bear on a second lorry even if it had not turned the corner. South of the road Stephen O'Neill had six men of No. 3 Section while the rest were well back from the road to the north of the ambush site in case even more lorries turned up. From there they could fire on the approach route. At nine in the morning they were in position, and there they waited. Another man, John Lordan, appeared and was allocated to No. 2 Section. They waited some more. The people in the house gave them what food they had, but there was not enough for all. They waited all through the day until the light began to fade

The ambush site at Kilmichael is marked with a memorial celebrating the success of Barry's Flying Column. The trucks came round the corner in the distance and were stopped on the road to the right where they came under fire from, amongst other places, snipers hiding behind the rocks in the immediate foreground.

when suddenly, round the corner from Kilmichael, came a cart pulled by a grey horse with five fully-armed IRA men. At the same time the signal of the Auxiliaries' approach arrived and the cart was sent at the gallop away down to the house.

The day before, Barry had borrowed from Paddy O'Brien his IRA officer's tunic. He had his own field equipment of British pattern. Thus clad, he stood in the middle of the road as the first truck drove swiftly round the corner. Puzzled by the appearance of an officer in the midst of the countryside in the fading light, the Crossley slowed. A hand grenade flew through the air to explode next to the driver, a whistle blew and gunfire began. The truck slowed to a halt and the fighting became hand-to-hand, revolvers and bayonets exploding and stabbing as every man fought savagely. The nine men who had been in the back of the lorry soon fell and Barry could see what was going on with the second truck. No. 2 Section was firing on a group of Auxiliaries who had leapt into the road and were lying there returning fire. After a while they shouted, 'We surrender.' Barry and his companions were creeping along the roadside to help and saw the Auxiliaries throw their rifles down. Then the men of the Flying Column stood up, one crouching and two upright. Immediately the firing resumed, with revolvers, and Barry saw one of his men fall and then another, Pat Deasy.

Barry was now only twenty-five yards behind his enemies and ordered rapid fire. Some of the Auxiliaries ran, others cried surrender, but none survived. Michael McCarthy was dead and so was Jim Sullivan. Young Pat Deasy was clearly dying. He was given first aid and a door was fetched to carry him away. The weapons and papers of the Auxiliaries were collected before the trucks were set on fire. They presented arms to the bodies of their fallen comrades before marching away, through renewed rain, to cross the River Bandon before British patrols could be deployed. Martial law was proclaimed on 10 December, and it was also alleged by the British that the bodies of the Auxiliaries had been mutilated. Barry sternly denied the allegation made in Field Marshal Lord French's proclamation, but neither of them saw the fallen on the Monday morning following and no one had mounted guard overnight. Perhaps it was a propaganda ploy, perhaps it was true that someone had mauled the corpses, but if that had been done Barry's Flying Column cannot be blamed.

The British army had severe doubts about the behaviour of the Auxiliaries. General Sir Nevil Macready wrote on the day martial law was declared that it would be necessary to watch the police very carefully as their reaction was likely to be that they could shoot anyone they did not like the look of. The next day an ambush was carried out by the IRA close to Victoria Barracks near Cork. That night men of K Company, an Auxiliary unit, went into town, apparently under the command of their officers, and set fire to a shop in St Patrick Street. More shops were soon on fire. The troops responsible for imposing the curfew took no action, and later it was claimed that if they had life would have been lost. As it was, the buildings along the southern side of St Patrick Street from Cook Street to Merchant's Quay were utterly destroyed and others damaged; scarcely 'half the town' as some claimed, but an amazing destruction carried out by those allegedly present to keep the peace.

Tom Barry recounts that, by March 1921, the British were operating in units some three hundred strong and that is why his Brigade Flying Column had been built up to one hundred and four officers and men, large enough to mount resistance should one of the British sweeps attempt to scoop them up. On 16 March Barry got the news that a force of about 300 men was to be sent from Kinsale to Bandon as reinforcements and he determined to ambush this British detachment. The Flying Column took up positions at Shippool, halfway along the route, on the east bank of the Bandon River where the road kinks in a little side valley. They waited in vain as the British set out but withdrew, presumably because they had news of the ambush. Barry pulled his men back to Skeugh on the high ground north west of Kinsale and 18 March was spent waiting in billets.

Between Bandon in the west and Cork in the east a road runs across the low land and another follows a route a little to the north, hard under the slopes of the hills, from the junction with the road to Crookstown north-east to Crossbarry and then east to Ballinhassig. On the night of 18 March Barry moved his men north of these roads to Ballyhandle, north west of Crossbarry, a place from which the low ground is overlooked. During the night reports came in of British troop movements and Barry lists these as follows: 400 left Cork, 200 Ballincollig, 300 Kinsale and 350 Bandon in the early hours and another 150 Auxiliaries left Macroom later. Yet more men are said to have marched as day approached. Something in the region of 1,500 are thus reported to have been deployed, north, west and south of Crossbarry. About half dismounted from their transport and began a sweep through houses and barns searching for IRA men. About three miles north of Crossbarry they succeeded in catching the West Cork Brigade Commandant, Charles Hurley, in a house in which he had been recovering from a gunshot wound. He died in an exchange of fire.

Barry was now in danger of being caught himself. It was very unlikely that the Flying Column could manage to slip away undetected, given that all roads of any size had both foot and truck-borne troops on them. Further, ammunition was down to about forty rounds per man, so a running fight could not be sustained. However, it seemed likely that the troops approaching from the west would reach Crossbarry before any others, so an ambush might succeed and open a line of retreat. The village is divided by the Aughnaboy River running from north to south through it and the main west-east road has two minor roads crossing it some thirty yards apart, the westerly one close to the river. The Flying Column was positioned to the west of all these and on the north of the main road, using the ditch for cover. The road turns south to Crossbarry Bridge before reaching the river and after that turn a stone wall was thrown up to delay the column. The minor road to the north was overlooked from the grounds of the old castle, Castlefield, and a section was positioned there to guard the flank and rear. Seventy-three officers and men were placed to attack and thirty-one were covering flanks and rear by 5.30 a.m. At about 8 o'clock a long line of trucks drove along the road from the west and when a dozen or so were within the attack zone a British soldier saw one of the Volunteers at a barn door. As the soldiers leapt from the trucks Barry's men opened fire. Those who were not hit made good their escape, and three sections were sent to chase them. They did not stop running until, Barry says, they reached the other Cork to Bandon road about one and a half miles away. Barry now chose to hold his ground instead of moving off to the south himself. His men grabbed ammunition and abandoned rifles and one man who had been an unwilling passenger in the convoy tottered forward with a Lewis machine-gun and eight full ammunition pans for it. Two further attacks from the south east and north east followed, but were fought off and finally a detachment crept down from the north west only to be brought under fire from Castlefield. Two hours had passed and Barry now withdrew his troops, leaving three dead and taking two seriously wounded with him to Gurranereigh, some fourteen miles to the west.

The impression Barry gives is of a landscape strewn with British dead and a mighty victory, but the most substantial figure claimed by republican writers is something in excess of thirty dead. Peter Hart points out that the internal police and military documents, supported by the findings of an inquest, state that ten men were killed and four wounded in this engagement. Given the fact that only part of the motorised column was engaged, and exclusively from the north, and that the remaining attacks were against positions by then known to the British, substantial casualties are not to be expected. Indeed, it would seem that marksmanship was not a common skill amongst a force that was firing, according to its leader, at ranges of only five to ten yards. Barry did well in selecting his positions and organising an ambush that broke the cordon with

The Crossbarry memorial.

The memorial on the site of the ambush of Michael Collins at Béal na mBláth.

which the British hoped to surround him, but in this, one of the very few fights of the time large enough to come within the scope of this book, the claim of a substantial victory over a force of more that 1,200 men rings hollow. The British, on the other hand, had little to boast about either. They had allowed a column of trucks to drive straight into an ambush and lost ten men in the process. They had also resupplied their enemies and lost a number of trucks set afire. Another failure in the guerilla war.

The conclusion of a treaty to bring the war to an end did not herald an age of quiet and harmony, for the Civil War followed. The action at the Four Courts in Dublin came to a dramatic conclusion with the government and Michael Collins having the upper hand. Collins would not survive long.

The anti-treaty IRA was particularly strong in Munster and the forces of the Provisional Government were vigorous in opposing their former comrades. Battles as such did not really form part of this war any more than they did in the previous one against the British, but the conflict was, if possible, even more bitter and vicious, including the casual killing of anyone suspected of being an informer, often on grounds of religion or mere dislike. Few such victims were guilty, as Peter Hart's chilling book has shown.

The motive for Michael Collins's journey to Cork in August 1922 was ostensibly to inspect the South-Western Command in an area of strong Republican resistance, but there is also some evidence that he planned to meet key figures in the Republican movement to seek resolution of their differences. The route selected itself exposed him to danger, taking his party in the early morning through the remote valley of Béal na mBláth, 'The Mouth of the Flowers', on the way to Bandon. There they stopped to ask the way, speaking to Dinny Long, a member of Cork No. 2 Brigade of the Republican IRA. When the convoy had passed on its way, plans were made to ambush Collins on the return journey.

The trap was set in expectation of Collins and his party making the trip back to Cork late that afternoon, but the time passed and no one came. At eight o'clock that evening the ambush party gave up, some of them making for the pub and five others clearing up the barricade and mine they had readied for the operation. As they did so they heard the sound of approaching vehicles and moved back into position. When fired upon, Collins threw himself into the battle instead of attempting to evade his enemies; there was ample opportunity for him to get away. The exchange of fire lasted for perhaps half an hour before the attackers were forced to withdraw, but by then Collins was severely wounded on the back of the neck and he died shortly after. Countless conflicting versions of the incident have circulated over the years, but the likelihood is that a ricochet was the cause of the wound.

Under the Anglo-Irish Treaty of December 1921, Article 6 declared that the defence of Britain and Ireland at sea remained the responsibility of the British, and so Bantry Bay remained a British naval port. That status ceased in 1938 and on 26 September the Irish army took over the installations. Since that day Munster has been at peace.

4

The
Western Flank

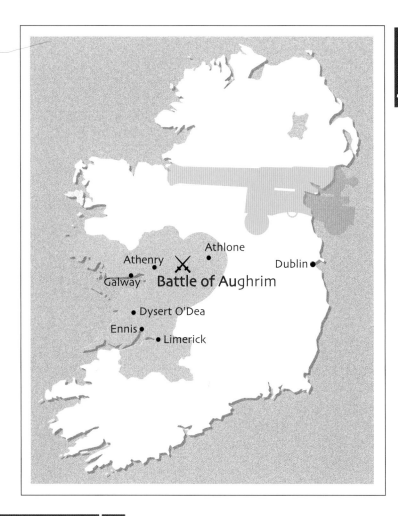

Athlone

Athenry ✕
Galway **Battle of Au**ghrim

Dublin •

• Dysert O'Dea
Ennis •
• Limerick

Much of the western coast of Ireland constitutes a daunting barrier to incomers from the sea, but two welcoming havens, the Shannon estuary and Galway Bay, were seen as points of vulnerability by those already in residence. The survival of the dramatic and beautiful drystone forts such as Dun Aengus, in the Aran Islands at the mouth of Galway Bay, suggest that even in prehistoric times the tenure of the natives was insecure. From Limerick, at the mouth of the Shannon, the chain of river and lough throws a great, watery shield running north and south to separate east from west, while between the Shannon estuary and Galway Bay a mass

Even in the apparently invader-unfriendly terrain of County Galway a crannóg in Lough Skannive, ringed in white stone, is needed to provide security from raiders.

The arms of the O'Malleys, the family of the famed pirate queen, Grace, on a tomb on Clare Island, County Mayo, bear the image of an early sailing galley.

of small loughs and rivers hampers the movement of a substantial force. North of Galway Bay the combination of mountain and broad lough has the same effect, leaving only Galway and Limerick as gateways to the interior and the crossings of the Shannon vital links in routes from east to west, so crucial to Britain-based armies, and from west to east for sea-borne troops.

Normans and Irish

The Viking settlement of Limerick in about A.D. 922 indicated the start of a more commercial relationship between the Ostmen and the Irish than that of the spasmodic raids of earlier years. The site was an island at the lowest crossing point over the river Shannon and it became the power centre of the kings of Thomond, north Munster, who extended their rule first to Munster as a whole and then, with Brian Boru, to the High Kingship of Ireland. Thus the descendants of Brian Boru, the O'Briens, came to rule in Limerick until displaced by the Anglo-Norman arrivals in the late twelfth century. But Norman domination was not complete and the O'Briens retained power in County Clare, immediately to the north. Galway, on the other hand, was a Norman construct, what small settlement there was being taken by Richard de

Limerick Castle, securing the entrance to the River Shannon.

Burgh in 1230. The region thus had two major Norman outposts at Limerick and Galway joined by a curving chain of castles and manors along the Shannon and east from Galway to Lough Ree; in fact, domination of the routes through the region.

A major destabilisation, if the recurrent round of minor wars of succession to chieftainships can be regarded as a stable situation, was caused by Edward Bruce's campaigns in Ireland after May 1315. His attacks on the English interest, or rather pursuit in Ireland of what was a Scots-Norman feud against an Anglo-Norman monarchy in England, also had the effect of loosening Anglo-Norman control of Irish rulers. On 10 August 1316, for instance, Fedlimidh Ua Conchobhair (Felim O'Connor) fought a mighty battle against the Anglo-Irish of Connacht under William de Burgh. It was an error, for he lost comprehensively amid scenes of great slaughter at Athenry, east of Galway. Raphael Holinshed's *Chronicles of England, Scotland and Ireland* gives an account of a meeting after the battle when the body of one O'Kelly was sought and the uncertain loyalties of the time are shown:

> But yet to the further scattering of the English forces in Ireland, there rose four
> princes of Connagh, but the Burghes and Birminghams discomfited them, and

slew eleven thousand of them beside Athenrie ... The lord Richard Birmingham had an esquier that belonged to him called John Husseie, who by the commandement of his maister went foorth to take view of the dead bodies and to bring him word whether Okellie his mortalle foe were slaine among the residue. Husseie comming into the field with one man to turne up and survey the dead carcases, was streight espied by Okellie, that lay lurking in a brake bush thereby, who having had good proof of Husseie's valor before that time, longed sore to train him from his capteine, and presuming now upon his good opportunitie, disclosed himselfe, not doubting, but either to win him with courteous persuasions, or by force to work his will of him, and so comming to him said: 'Husseie, thou seest that I am at all points armed, and have my esquire here likewise furnished with armour and weapon readie at mine elbow; thou art naked [that is, unarmed] with thy page, a yoongling, and not to be accounted of: so that if I loved thee not, and meant to spare thee for mine own sake, I might now doo with thee what I would, and slay thee for thy master's sake. But come and serve me upon this request here made to thee, and I promise thee by St Patrick's staff to make thee a lord in Connagh, of more possessions than thy master hath in Ireland.' When these words might were said, his own man (a great stout lubber) began to reprove him of folie, for not consenting to so large an offer ...

Hussey acted at once. He turned and killed his own squire and then caught O'Kelly's

Carrigogunnel Castle, an O'Brien stronghold built on a rock outcrop on the southern shore of the Shannon Estuary. Some parts date back to the late thirteenth century.

man such a blow under his ear that he fell unconscious. Then he went for O'Kelly himself and slew him. The Irishman's squire came to, and Hussey had him bear his late master's head on a trencher before him to present it to Birmingham. For this feat and his loyalty Hussey was knighted and richly rewarded. At Athenry the Irish lost to an Anglo-Irish alliance, but further south two years later the result was very different. The rule of Thomond was in dispute between two branches of the O'Briens from the late thirteenth century onward. A brief truce when it was split between Turlough (Toirdhealbhach) O'Brien and Donough (Donnchadh) O'Brien ended when the former killed the latter in 1284. In 1317 the two sides were still fighting and Turlough's successor, Murtough (Muircheartach), won a victory over another Donough at Corcomroe Abbey, in the Burren Hills on the southern side of Galway Bay. Now Brian O'Brien allied himself with Richard de Clare, titular lord of Thomond under a grant of Edward I. De Clare perhaps saw this as a chance to make his lordship real by siding with the aspirant to Murtough's domain.

The conflict was stimulated by Murtough's raiding of de Clare's cattle. The Anglo-Norman lord moved up from his castle at Bunratty together with his few knights and a force of footmen, probably spearmen and archers, drawn from his tenantry who owed him feudal service. The knights were probably mounted on the native, light, horses and would no longer be of the heavy, shock-troop type of earlier days. Also with him were Brian O'Brien's foot soldiers. They sought their adversaries amongst the woods, streams and loughs that so much favour ambush. De Clare moved north past Quin, south east of Ennis, where a former de Clare castle, by then lost and damaged, stood. In its day it had been a modern structure – four corner turrets with curtain walls between them. The simplicity of the square design was probably its downfall, for although attackers breaking into the courtyard would come under fire from the walltop archers, it was as hard to make an undetected sally as it had been from a motte and thus static resistance was the only option. A Franciscan friary later made use of the ruins in a new edifice. From Quin de Clare moved north to Ruan and thence, on the morning of 10 May 1318, westwards. He now entered the lands of Conor O'Dea, one of Murtough's allies.

De Clare divided his force into three, taking the centre himself and sending the other two north and south of the line he was riding, plundering and sacking the country as they went. The fourteenth century account, *Cathréim Thoirdhealbhaigh (The Triumphs of Turlough)*, then tells of a remarkable meeting with an ancient woman as they crossed the river Fergus:

> ... that in the current washed and with huge exertion dipped old armours, satin vestments, goldthreaded jacks of price, smooth finetextured silken shirts, handsome oversea-fashioned wares, with other garments and strippings of a host; so that all of the river below her was made a broo of blood and water ...

De Clare sends a Gaelic speaker to quiz the wench, who tells them that she is washing the clothes and accoutrements of de Clare, his sons, knights, squires and Gaelic allies, for that day they will all be with her in hell. De Clare dismisses the warning with the

A carving of Christ's resurrection on the MacMahon tomb at Ennis Friary, dating from about 1475, shows knights in contemporary plate armour with conical helmets and armed with axes.

arguments first, that witches always lie, and second, that Sir William Burke is on his way to reinforce them. In terms of effective military reconnaissance the tale is unreliable, but it adds a certain zest.

O'Dea then tried diplomacy but de Clare would not accept tribute, according to *The Triumphs*, and was forced to plan a holding action until Fedlimidh Ua Conchobhair and Lochlainn O'Hechir could come to support him. As he rode south west towards Dysert, where the destruction of O'Dea's house was his objective, de Clare came across a party of the enemy near Lough Ballycullinan. They were driving a herd of cattle across a ford and turned to oppose the Norman-Irish. A hard contest ensued and then O'Dea began a fighting retreat, past the location of the modern Macken Bridge, where they stood again for a while, and across the Ennis to Corofin road into an area bounded on the south by woods and on the north by the lough. Richard de Clare led his men and the followers came as quickly as they could make progress against resistance at the ford. De Clare and his immediate supporters were cut down, but the rest kept coming and forced O'Dea's men into the woods where they were surrounded.

Just in time Fedlimidh Ua Conchobhair came roaring out of the west, over the hill of Scool, and cut his way through to rescue the O'Deas but more Normans from the flanking columns arrived and joined the fray. The casualties appear to have been

View to the south west over Lough Ballyculinan to the site of the battle of Dysert O'Dea.

heavy. De Clare's son and Fedlimidh Ua Conchobhair met and fought until the Norman was 'converted ... into a disfigured corpse'. Still the issue was in the balance, but Murtough O'Brien then arrived by way of Spancil Hill from the north east. At first the Irish took them for Burke's Norman reinforcements, which suggests both sides were, by this period, similarly armed and dressed. But the Normans now found themselves trapped between two Irish armies. The 'pale English' as *The Triumph* terms the Norman leaders, were killed to a man and their followers attempted to extricate themselves, pursued by the Irish who were victorious in, for them, the unusual circumstances of a long drawn-out, hand-to-hand battle. The chase took them as far as Bunratty Castle which they found already on fire, for the newly widowed Lady de Clare had taken ship for Limerick, destroying all she could not take with her. The de Clares never returned and the O'Briens became the undisputed rulers of Thomond – or rather Murtough did and Brian did not. The castle now standing at Bunratty is a tower house built in 1460 and restored in the 1950s.

The battles of Athenry and Dysert O'Dea showed the Irish fighting in a new way. Rather than the raid, ambush and hit-and-run warfare well suited to small numbers of men in wooded or mountainous terrain, the soldiers had fought in a mass, toe-to-toe with their adversaries. The new style of warfare made demands on manpower that the generally individualistic Irish found hard to meet in attitude, in numbers

A tomb at Roscommon Friary, now with the earlier effigy of Fedlimidh Ua Conchobhair (Felim O'Connor) on it, has this panel of a mail-clad man with conical helmet and short sword, while another such figure carries an axe. It is probably a depiction of a gallowglass.

and in the nature of their obligations; short terms of service being the limit of their duty. The need was met by importing fighting men from Scotland, first as specialist bodyguards but then increasingly as mercenaries available for hire for as long as needful and the funds held out. These gall óglach or gallowglass – foreign warriors – were granted land in the territory controlled by their sponsors and thus the clans of MacSweeney, MacDonald, MacCabe, MacSheehey and MacLeod established themselves in Ireland. Their weapons were the long-hafted axe, on occasion the short-handled axe, the spear and the two-handed sword, though axes were typical. They wore mail and conical helmets and were the most ferocious of warriors. In action two boys accompanied each fighting man to carry his provisions and his darts, the light throwing spears used to wound and slow the enemy, rather than to kill, before they came to blows. Eighty gallowglass with their attendants, 240 men in all, made up one battalion. They distinguished themselves at Knockdoe, the hill of the axes.

The Renewal of English Power

The Wars of the Roses in England kept monarchs and aspiring monarchs busy on their own side of the water, but with the eventual victory of Henry Tudor and his emergence as Henry VII, things changed. The king wished to regain control over Ireland, in part to guard against challenges to his tenure of the throne – Lambert Simnel's rebellion of 1487 took place only two years after he became king – and also to establish a flow of revenue into his vacant coffers. He had to come to terms with the fact that the former Yorkist, Gerald FitzGerald, Gearóid Mór, eighth Earl of Kildare, a man who had been present at Simnel's coronation in Dublin and whom he had imprisoned in the Tower of London in 1495, was a necessary adjunct to his rule in Ireland. The Earl of Kildare did not want to be king, he wanted to be the boss in Ireland, and therefore, through him, Henry could rule. In 1498 an attempt was made to outlaw private wars between chiefs in Ireland. It was forbidden to use their war-cries and to employ such typically Irish weapons as the spear or the dart, and Gearóid Mór had the responsibility for enforcing this. In 1503 Ulick Burke of Clanrickard, a MacWilliam feuding with the Mayo branch of the same family, attacked his cousin's allies, the O'Kellys and the next year destroyed three of their castles. Ulick was also Gearóid Mór's son-in-law and, it is said, was ill-treating his wife. At the same time Melaghlin O'Kelly appealed for protection against Burke. Gearóid Mór determined to deal with Burke. Turlough O'Brien came to the aid of Ulick Burke, whose mother was an O'Brien. Ulick's first wife had been a Macnamara, so they joined him too. The O'Carrolls and O'Kennedys were against the Earl of Kildare in any circumstance, and also joined Burke.

Gearóid Mór himself was certainly taking it seriously. Chief amongst his supporters in this quarrel were the O'Neills, or at least that faction that Gearóid Mór himself was backing in the dispute over who should be Earl of Tyrone. The O'Kellys, who had asked Gearóid Mór to get involved in the first place, were on good terms with the O'Donnells and they in turn brought the O'Connors along. A great posse of chiefs rallied to Gearóid Mór: Magennis, MacMahon, O'Hanlon, O'Reilly and O'Farrell. Further, as he was acting on behalf of the king, Gearóid Mór had the royal troops at his command, maybe about eighty Englishmen, and the men of the Pale, the muster of Prestons, Plunketts, Darcys, and other Anglo-Irish lords. Thus the Pale, Ulster, north Connacht and the Midlands were with Gearóid Mór and the west and south-west, Clare and Munster, were with Burke. It is interesting to note that in early accounts of the conflict the former were called English and the latter were seen as Irish. It is, of course, entirely misleading as almost everyone there was Irish and, as is clear from the loyalties that brought the two armies into being, more concerned with family and local loyalties than with the affairs of the king, even if they gave a pretext for war.

In the early summer of 1504 Ulick entered the town of Galway. This was in breach of the town's charter and ignited the fuse of battle. In August Gearóid Mór's army moved westwards. At about three o'clock in the afternoon on the day before the battle they halted some twenty miles east of Knockdoe to take counsel. Richard of Delvin was brief and bellicose; he was impatient to get at the enemy and swore to hurl the first spear – a weapon his side were supposed to eschew. Others wavered and claimed their adversaries had too many men and that 'a good giving back were better than a evil standing' but St Lawrence of Howth pointed out it was too late for that as the enemy was in sight. Gearóid Mór brought the discussion to a close by summoning the leader of his gallowglass, who reacted enthusiastically to being asked to open the battle, stimulating others to vie for the honour.

They marched further west before camping and on the morning of 19 August took up position on the gentle slopes of the hill, somewhat to the east of a low, stone wall and facing roughly west. The billmen, with their long-handled blades rather like agricultural billhooks, formed the centre of the line with archers on either side. The wall gave a certain protection from the centre to the right of the line, so the cavalry were positioned on the left to have freedom of movement. The gallowglass held the right flank and the baggage was to the rear.

Ulick also had gallowglass amongst his men, namely the MacSweeneys of Clanrickard and of Thomond who were about to oppose the O'Donnells and O'Neills, served by gallowglass MacSweeneys and MacDonalds respectively. It was all the same to them as professional soldiers; they were under contract. Ulick formed his foot soldiers into a solid block with gallowglass on either side. His cavalry was on his left. In all he had, perhaps, 4,000 men and his enemies half as many again, giving them, in theory, the advantage.

Ulick's gallowglass charged forward and Gearóid Mór's archers made immediate reply with arrows. Then the two bodies of men came together and hacked and slashed at each other for hours on end. There is no suggestion in the sparse report from that time of any attempt at manoeuvre. Gearóid Mór's son, who had been given command of the reserve and charged with the protection of the baggage, could not contain himself. *The Book of Howth*, a mid-sixteenth century document, says:

> The young Gerotte this being time for relief, seeing the battle joining, could not

The gentle slopes of Knockdoe Hill were the scene of the great battle between Ulick Burke and Gerald FitzGerald (Gearóid Mór), eighth Earl of Kildare.

stand still to wait his time as he was appointed by the Earl his father, but set on with the foremost in such sort that no man alive could do better with his own hands than he did that day, for manhood of a man; but by reason of his lustiness not tarrying in the place appointed, all the English carriages was taken away by the Irish horsemen, and a few of the English gentlemen take prisoners.

More detail we do not have, except for the intelligence that one of Ulick's men was killed with a new instrument of war when he blundered into Gearóid Mór's camp thinking they had surrendered. '... one of the Skquyvors, a soldier out of Dublin, strack him with a gun with both hands, and so beat out his brains.'

Eventually the flow went against Ulick and his men. Chroniclers report that nine battalions of gallowglass were reduced to less than one, which would suggest casualties of 2,000 or so, half of the army Ulick brought to the field. Perhaps it is true. In any case his force fell back towards Galway, defiantly promising a fresh battle, but instead they dispersed. Local stories exist of rear-guard actions at river crossings which may also be true. The known outcome is that Gearóid Mór, the Earl of Kildare, entered Galway without further resistance and rewarded his men with thirty tuns (large barrels) of wine.

Fights along the Shannon

Clonmacnoise, on the Shannon south of Athlone, is famed as the burial place of the kings of Connacht and Tara as well as being the site of the monastery founded by St Ciarán in A.D. 545, but it is equally the site of a castle guarding an important river crossing. The site on the east bank was fortified in the eleventh century as a ringwork, a circular bank, doubtless with some sort of palisade on top of it, approached by a causeway. It was probably constructed on the site of an even earlier fort, emphasising the importance of the river not only as a means of transportation in early times, but as a barrier to movement until the invention of the aircraft. At the time of construction it secured the river crossing on the *Eiscir Riada*, the principal east to west route along the ridge left by the Ice Age icecap's meltwater deposits. Early in the thirteenth century, certainly before 1215 when Ralph Derevaus and Walter Reboth were asked to yield it to Geoffrey de Marisco, a two-storey, rectangular keep and courtyard was constructed within the enclosure with a fore-building to protect its first-floor entrance. It seems likely that to get into the castle you had to pass along the face of the northern wall of the keep before negotiating the pit and drawbridge so the residents could observe you well in advance of your arrival. The function of the castle was, it appears, to oppose those coming from the west. In the Williamite Wars the threat was from the east.

After the Battle of the Boyne in July 1690, James II fled to France and the Jacobite force as a whole was soon behind the Shannon and holding the ports of Cork and Kinsale on the south coast. William of Orange moved against Limerick, but in August Patrick Sarsfield led an audacious raid on his artillery train, depriving him of a

The castle at Clonmacnois, guarding the river crossing on the Shannon.

significant proportion of his guns so that the attempt on the town was unsuccessful. The determination of the French commander, the Marquis de Boisseleau, and the courage of the Irish defenders, coupled with the miserable weather that sapped Williamite morale, led to the raising of the siege in September. John Churchill, Earl of Marlborough, took Cork and Kinsale by the end of October and the fighting season closed with the Jacobites well established west of the Shannon from Limerick to Athlone.

This war was, of course, just part of a larger European conflict in which the French king, Louis XIV, was a prime mover. The French fleet, having brushed off the attempted intervention of the English under Arthur Herbert, now Earl of Torrington, were still threatening the English coast. They were commanded by the formidably competent Comte de Tourville and while William was still in Ireland the diarist, John Evelyn, wrote:

> 27 June [1690]. I went to visit some friends in the Tower [of London where suspected Jacobites were interned], when asking for Lord Clarendon, they by mistake directed me to the Earl of Torrington, who about three days before had been sent for from the fleete, and put into the Tower for cowardice and not fighting the French fleete, which having beaten a squadron of the Hollanders, whilst Torrington did nothing, did now ride masters of the sea, threatening a descent.

> 3 August. The French landed some souldiers at Teinemouth in Devon, and burnt some poore houses … The French fleete still hovering about the Western coast, and we having 300 sail of rich merchant ships in the bay of Plymouth, our fleete moving towards them, under three Admirals. The country in the West all on their guard.

> 15 September. The unseasonable and most tempestuous weather happening, the naval expedition is hinder'd and the extremity of wet causes the siege of Limerick to be rais'd. K. William returned to England. Lord Sydney was left governor of what is conquer'd in Ireland, which is three parts [i.e. three quarters].

The Williamites did not, in fact, rest that winter. Where they could inch forward, they did. On the Shannon Major-General James Douglas moved west towards Sligo but his attempts to cross the river at Lanesborough, at the northern end of Lough Ree from Athlone, failed when a Colonel Ulick Burke won the day, and at Jamestown, further north near Carrick-on-Shannon, were frustrated by the nimble Major-General Sarsfield. Sarsfield had also fortified Ballymore, halfway between Athlone and the Williamite headquarters at Mullingar, but the wisdom of this is doubted by Hayes-McCoy as is Sarsfield's strategic, as opposed to tactical, competence. James II's commander, the Earl of Tyrconnell, returned to Ireland in January 1691 and in May the French sent fresh supplies to Limerick, as well as a new, independent field commander, Lieutenant-General the Marquis de St Ruth, but no more soldiers. The Jacobite forces amounted to perhaps 20,000 men.

William's forces were commanded by Lieutenant-General Godart van Ginkel, who was to become the first Earl of Athlone. He brought his forces together at Mullingar in May. There were men from Ulster as well as Dutch, Danish, French Huguenot and English soldiers present. Ginkel had more than thirty siege guns, six mortars and twelve field guns. In all there were some 25,000 men. Their first objective was the garrison at Ballymore, and here for a second time in history an Ulick Burke was facing a force from the east. The colonel had 500 men to hold the place but they stood, nonetheless, while, on 7 June, Ginkel's cannon opened fire. The Reverend George Story, who was a padre with the Williamite army, wrote:

> All our guns and mortars fell to work ... the bombs tearing up the sandy banks, and the Irish running like conies [rabbits] from one hole to another, whilst the guns were batering the works and making a breach, the Irish in the meantime did what they could with their two guns and small shot; but Lieutenant-Col. Burton, their engineer, had his hand shot off from one of our batteries, and their works went down apace which made the Irish very uneasy.

And who would not be uneasy under such an assault? Eventually Burke raised a white flag and Ginkel, at seven o'clock on the evening of 8 June, accepted the surrender. The resulting two-day delay was insignificant in the perfection of the Athlone defences and the loss of good troops cannot have helped the Jacobite cause.

The Jacobite approach to the defence of Athlone was to withdraw all but two or three regiments from the eastern side of the river, prepare the nine-arch bridge of that time for closure by demolition of two arches and build earthworks at both ends of the structure. On 20 June the artillery bombardment began. St Ruth rotated his troops in the east of the river to keep them fresh, but with masonry cascading about them and heavy fire from Ginkel's men, the position could not be held. They retired to the west and left a broken bridge behind them. The artillery fire continued for another week and Ginkel's men worked their way forward. Using fascines – bundles of wood – as cover, they managed to get planks across the gaps in the bridge and prepared to assault the barricade at the far end. On the Jacobite side men were called for to throw down the planks and out of the ranks one Sergeant Custume led ten men to do so. In the withering musket fire they were all killed before they could finish the job, but another twenty men led by a lieutenant replaced them and finished the work. Only two survived. Their heroism saved the town; for the time being.

Another effort to cross the bridge was made the next day but the cover and fascines were set afire by the Jacobites. A new idea was needed and Major-General Thomas Tollemache came up with one. First, he tried an experiment. There were three Danish soldiers guilty of some infringement and requiring punishment. They were to be sent over the river protected with 'front-armour', breastplates, wading through the river, which was as low as anyone could remember. To protect them it was pretended they were deserters and muskets were fired over their heads for effect. The men returned hardly hurt at all, so a serious attack was planned. At six in the evening Major-General Hugh MacKay led a storming party onto the bridge under heavy covering fire while

The River Shannon is now tamed with weirs and locks, but the crossing at Athlone would be formidable to a land army even today. From this viewpoint the west bank is to the left.

The site of the Battle of Aughrim. The Williamites approached from the left where the line of the old road curls towards the viewer from the modern carriageway. To the left and down from the church, on the nearer side of the road, a white-topped shed stands in the field where the remains of the castle and the Memorial Cross now stand. To the right, on the other side of the main road beyond the yellow building, one road forks right past a pale field on the way to Limerick while the other fork, to the left, leads to Tristaun Bridge. This road approximates the Jacobite front line.

below the tallest grenadiers advanced, led by the German officer serving with the Danes, Major-General Tettau. They stormed into the town, put down the resistance at the west end of the bridge and cleared Athlone in half an hour. Next day the castle surrendered and the Shannon was crossed. St Ruth retired to Ballinasloe and prepared to fight further to the south west on the road to Loughrea at the village of Aughrim.

At that time the position was better suited to a defensive action than it is today. The Ballinasloe to Loughrea road crosses the valley of the river Melehan which flows roughly north to south to join Tristaun Stream running east. It was a boggy valley bottom through which the Melehan ran, and after the road came over the bridge it was confined to a curving, narrow causeway to pass under the ruinous walls of Aughrim Castle, across another little rivulet and up the slope through Aughrim village. Beyond the village the road forks, one route due south leading to Limerick (and this splits to give a road south east towards Laurencetown) and the other to the south west going to Loughrea and Galway. The Laurencetown road runs along the

Urraghry Hill seen from the Jacobite line, looking across the remains of the bog. The landscape appears very different from the aerial impression.

ridge above the bog before it dips to cross the Tristaun Stream and rises through the Pass of Urraghry – pass in this instance meaning a place one can travel through rather than a defile through hills. This road was a way to approach the Jacobite right wing while the Ballinasloe road went for the left wing of the position chosen by St Ruth amongst the little hedge-outlined fields of Kilcommadan Hill. The hills are not high nor the slopes steep but this mild, gentle countryside was to become a killing ground.

The Jacobite army had Sarsfield's cavalry on the extreme right covering the ford over the Tristaun on the Laurencetown road with what became known as Bloody Hollow, where the road dips, on their left. In front of them were infantry and dragoons. The infantry, in two lines, the foremost between the road to Aughrim village and the bog, positioned in the little fields, while the second line in more formal style with musketeers in front and pikemen behind, stood approximately on the road itself. At the village cavalry and dragoons faced the slope up from the causeway and in the castle were two hundred musketeers.

Ginkel had left Athlone on 7 July and reached the River Suck near Ballinasloe four days later. He came on cautiously, not knowing exactly where St Ruth was. On 12 July, a foggy Sunday, the Williamites moved forward and, early in the afternoon, some of

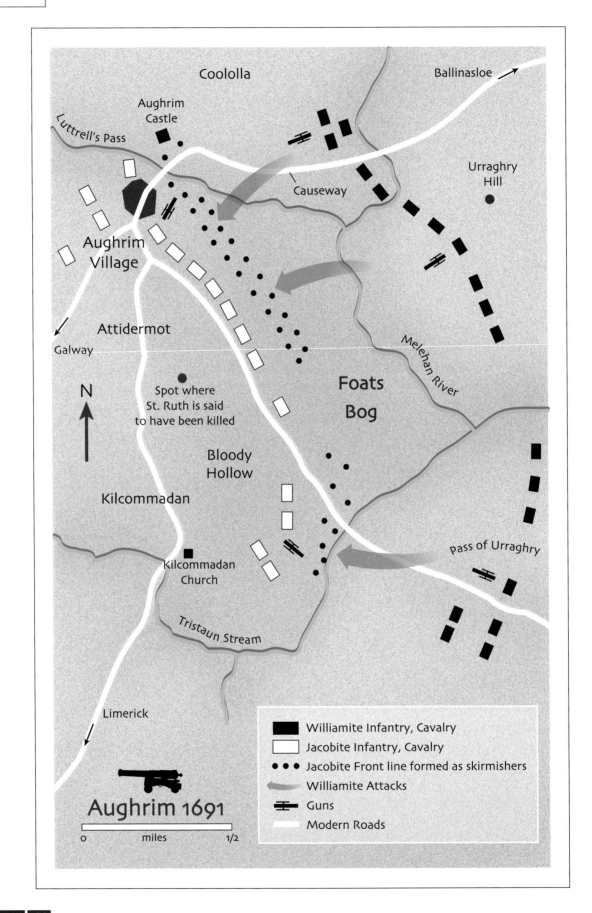

Coololla

Ballinsloe

Aughrim Castle

Luttrell's Pass

Causeway

Urraghry Hill

Aughrim Village

Attidermot

Galway

Melehan River

N

Spot where St. Ruth is said to have been killed

Foats Bog

Bloody Hollow

Kilcommadan

Kilcommadan Church

Pass of Urraghry

Tristaun Stream

Limerick

Aughrim 1691

0   miles   1/2

	Williamite Infantry, Cavalry
	Jacobite Infantry, Cavalry
•••	Jacobite Front line formed as skirmishers
	Williamite Attacks
	Guns
	Modern Roads

his Danish cavalry ran into some of St Ruth's mounted sentinels. The movement developed in the direction of Tristaun Stream and Ginkel, coming to a position on the southern flank of Urraghry Hill, found he could see along the valley to Aughrim village and survey much of the Jacobite line. It appeared that an opportunity existed to attack St Ruth's right beyond the Tristaun ford. The Williamite army was forming in the pre-arranged positions, with cavalry in the north by the Ballinasloe road, Major-General MacKay's English infantry in the front line to their left with Tollemache's English and Ulster infantry behind him, Tettau's Huguenots and Danes to MacKay's left with Count Nassau's Dutch and Danes to his rear and more cavalry and dragoons on the extreme left. It was now about four o'clock in the afternoon.

The castle mound at Aughrim.

Ginkel and his officers consulted. Some thought it too late to fight that day, but others pointed out that St Ruth seemed to be moving men to his right and MacKay suggested, in consequence, that immediate action might succeed at the northern end of the line, near the castle. At about five the assault on the Tristaun ford began with more dragoons taken from the Williamite right to reinforce it. St Ruth countered by moving some infantry from his centre to his right. MacKay's men then attempted to advance across the uncertain, boggy ground at the northern end of the valley and had some success, a few of them establishing themselves behind hedges there, but most of them were thrust back and one Jacobite unit, commanded by Gordon O'Neill, even took a Williamite gun. The Tristaun ford was eventually forced and slow, painful progress was made across land cut by hedge and ditch, all the time with the threat of the Irish cavalry on the hill above should the infantry rush forward too far. The Huguenots led by La Mellionière got across the bog and, using stakes they set in the ground, stubbornly stood against all attack, giving Bloody Hollow its name.

Evening was coming on; it was about half-past six. The causeway was too narrow a pass, so MacKay's infantry struggled through the bog, often waist-deep in mud and water. They had no alternative but to advance on the hedges before them once they emerged and managed to clear the first of them. The fight became one of hedgerows and as they fought forward the English were dismayed to find that St Ruth had arranged for gaps to be cut before the battle began and through these gaps the Irish cavalry galloped in amongst them. It was as if the forest and defile conditions of ancient warfare had been recreated with bog, hedge and ditch setting the English up for an Irish ambush all over again. Back the English tumbled and splashed, with serious loss. A stalemate was now becoming possible with the Williamite attacks on both wings stalled.

It was on the northern, the village, end of the front that the break came. MacKay sent two regiments of infantry, Kirk's and Gustavus Hamilton's, against the castle position. Then two more, Bellasis's and George Hamilton's, got over below the village and barricaded the hedge-gap against cavalry. Four regiments were now on firm ground west of the river and bog. South of that success more infantry attempted to cross the bog and suffered at the hands of Irish troops positioned behind the walls and hedges, falling back in a welter of blood to the delight of St Ruth on the hillside above. Tollemache rallied the retreating men, added the last of his reserve, and returned to the fray, back over the foul, bloody bog once more and with the whole of the infantry now over the bog, it was time for cavalry. Story described the infantry's determination in partisan terms.

> The English marched boldly up to their old ground again from whence they had been so lately beat; which is only natural to an Englishman, for it is observable that they are commonly fiercer and bolder after being repulsed than before, and what blunts the courage of all other nations commonly whets theirs; I mean the killing of their fellow-soldiers before their faces.

MacKay had cavalry on his right, but they hesitated to risk riding two by two over the causeway. The general tried first and was thrown from his mount. Then the Huguenot, the Marquis de Ruvigny, took the lead and the men followed, costly though it was. Oxford's Royal Regiment of Horse Guards, later to become the Blues, followed to clear ground for yet more and soon the Williamite cavalry was on firm ground on St Ruth's left. The infantry could now resume their advance and St Ruth had to take action. He sent orders for his cavalry on that wing to attack, putting himself at the head of a troop of the Life Guard and, pausing only to direct fire from one of his few guns, made ready to sweep Ginkel's men off the northern end of the field. At that moment a cannon-ball took off his head. A self-proclaimed witness of very doubtful veracity said, 'I see his hat fly off and his head is in it.'

The Irish left collapsed. St Ruth's second-in-command, the Marquis de Tessé, led a cavalry charge, but already the news of the general's death was spreading and men were turning away from the fight. The Williamite cavalry did not find the resistance they expected and, from north to south, the Jacobites fell away. The infantry held in the centre for a while, but without cavalry they could not endure and then those of Ginkel's men so long held up at Tristaun ford found they could advance. Darkness and rain covered the field and in it horsemen hunted down fleeing infantry. The destruction of the Jacobite army was comprehensive; about 4,000 of them were killed, twice the number of their enemies' fatalities. John Evelyn wrote:

> 19 July ... The greate victory of K. William's army in Ireland was look'd on as decisive of that war. The French General Saint Ruth, who had been so cruel to

The stone installations for the traversing rail for the cannon, which had a pivot to the left, on Carrig Island. Across the Shannon estuary in the distance (left) Scattery Island commanded the northern shore.

the poore Protestants in France, was slain, with divers of the best Commanders; nor was it cheape to us, having 1000 kill'd, but of the enemy 4 or 5000.

Ginkel moved on to Galway. The town yielded itself to him on 24 July and the garrison was permitted to leave. It took some time to turn to Limerick and it was 25 August before the Williamites arrived. They brought with them twenty-nine 'tynne' boats, presumably metal-sheathed boats as listed in the artillery train before the Battle of the Boyne, and the intention was to use them for a pontoon bridge. The scheme was successful when the grenadiers led by Brigadier Tiffin and some cavalry crossed the Shannon to surprise Colonel Clifford's camp. He was then able to circle from east to west around St Thomas's Island to attack the Thomond Bridge. The drawbridge was raised at once, leaving 600 Irish soldiers at the mercy of the Williamites, which they found minimal. The surrender was agreed on 3 October, its terms too lenient on the Catholics in the eyes of Ireland's Protestants and too favourable to the Protestants in the eyes of the Catholics.

Closing the Western Door

During the early part of the eighteenth century military activity in Ireland was minimal, but with the Bantry Bay expedition it became clear once more that invasion was a real danger. In December 1796 *L'Indomptable* had cruised off the Shannon waiting for the rest of the French to join her from Bantry Bay. They never came, but

The fortification of the approaches to Galway pre-dated the Napoleonic structures. This bastioned fort on the island of Inisbofin was listed as having cost £1,000 in 1664 and the structure on which it was based was one of the last Irish posts to surrender in 1653. It is built on what is said to be the site of a castle built by a pirate named Bosco, and is now known, for no good reason, as Cromwell's Fort.

the need for defence was evidently pressing. The Shannon estuary narrows at Tarbert and here, in 1794, in response to the outbreak of war in 1793, two batteries were begun. By 1815 an impressive array of signal stations and batteries had been constructed. General Dumouriez's memorandum of 1808 proposed batteries on either side of the estuary at its mouth and the structure at Kilcredaun Point on the north was a direct result. The fortification of Scattery Island was another of his suggestions as was the battery at Kilkerin Point, opposite the existing installation at Tarbert Island.

The design of most of these batteries was the same. A curved parapet faced the area to be protected or attacked, making a D-shaped structure. Six guns were intended to fire over the broad, low wall and to the rear, on the straight side, was a rectangular blockhouse. The whole was surrounded with a dry moat. The blockhouse was called a defensible guardhouse in contemporary writings and was given loop-holes for defence by musketeers and had a flat-topped roof which could also be manned. The fortlet was thus intended to dominate the waterway with cannon fire and also to be fit to endure a small siege if need be. Kilkerin Point Battery remains in sound condition and the field of fire the twenty-four-pounder guns would have commanded can be appreciated. Its sister installation on Tarbert Island across the water has been displaced by a power station. Of an earlier design, it was bastion-shaped, that is a square with arrow-head-shaped corners, and having two sides overlooking the water. The older structures were also used. Clare Castle had brick-edged musket loops which were probably added at this time and the modification of Limerick Castle to take contemporary artillery had results which can be seen today. The gatehouse towers were rebuilt to take the modern cannon and the parapets changed to give room for them to traverse.

Galway Bay was the alternative entry-point for an invader in the west. North of the bay the mountains and loughs offered too great a challenge to the movement of troops en masse and the next suitable location was Killala where General Humbert landed with his French army in 1798. At the mouth of Galway Bay the Aran Islands were furnished with signal towers, one on Inishmore and the other on Inisheer, with towers on the mainland to the south at Hogs Head and to the north at Golam Head. A report of 1798 identified possible landing places at Oranmore, east of Galway town, and at Ballyvaughan Bay on the southern shore near the Burren. A Martello tower was built at Finavarra Point to protect the latter. It is cam-shaped in plan and mounted three guns, each sitting in a semi-circular emplacement on top of the three-curved cam when seen from above. It was entered, as was usual, by a ladder to the first floor which has four windows. The associated battery, now gone, had another three, or perhaps

The blockhouse on Carrig Island on the south shore of the Shannon Estuary.

Aughinish Martello tower on the south shore of Galway Bay.

four, guns. Another, similar, installation was put up east of there, at Aughinish. At a rather unlikely landing place on the north shore of Galway Bay, Casla Bay, a one- or two-gun tower was built at Rosaveel and manned by an officer and thirty men.

Between Galway and Limerick the River Shannon itself supplied the line of defence. The waterway was not a simple river-bed flowing briskly to the sea, but a complex of navigable channels, shallow streams, islands and loughs which offer both a line of defence and a porous border, one that could be infiltrated secretly. It is not, therefore, a simple thing to defend. In some stretches no defence was needed as it clearly could only be crossed by boat or is so shallow and unreliable that it could not be crossed at all. Elsewhere it was bridged and demanded attendant fortifications. Much has changed since the early nineteenth century with new channels and locks making navigation easy but obscuring the former nature of the military problems, so some imagination and local research is needed to get a clear picture.

Colonel Charles Tarrant of the Royal Irish Engineers went to work in June 1793 inspecting the potential strong-point at Athlone and there followed, three years later, recommendations for fortification at Lanesborough, Banagher and Portumna as well. It was the fresh outbreak of war in 1803 that gave the effective stimulus to build the forts of which evidence can be found today. To find some of them it is necessary to try very hard indeed, for some of the relics are unremarked and, apparently, uncared for. Others

The bulk of Meelick Martello tower, shrouded in greenery, stands on the island west of Victoria lock on the River Shannon.

are excellently preserved. The Meelik Martello tower has, or had when Paul Kerrigan inspected it in researching his book, the pivots and rails of the traversing platforms still in place as well as the ringbolts for the block and tackle used to turn the platforms from side to side. This tower, now with Victoria Lock to the south and the canal to the east, was intended to cover the ford and another ford, upstream at Keelogue, was also defended. Here a battery very much like those on the estuary was built. It differed in being half of a hexagon, rather than curved, in plan at the front. The front-pivoted traversing platform arrangements can be seen, seven of them, inside the broad parapet.

The most fascinating of these, in the event, unused fortifications is at Shannonbridge, yet further upstream. Here is a classic *tête-de-pont*, a bridgehead in the true sense, of which type of construction no other exists in the British Isles. It worked as a murderous arrowhead carrying massive guns at its point and aimed in the face of an enemy approaching from Ballinasloe. Considering it from the east, the bridge crosses the river to reach the broad end of the arrowhead where the road passes a river-side wall between a small arms battery to the right and a barrack block on the left into a sunken yard. Today the widened road swings in a curve to the left through an enlarged gap in the curtain wall before straightening up to head westwards, but when it was built it turned through an abrupt angle to pass out of a gate; the matching gate on the north side is still there. Anyone attempting to assault the closed gate would come under fire from the barrack on the east and from the back of the arrowhead redoubt on the west.

The redoubt, the stone-built part of the arrowhead itself, is set in a dry moat all exposed to fire from the lower levels of the fortification, and in front is the long slope of the glacis which guarantees that anyone approaching is exposed to fire from the guns mounted on the redoubt. Down in the dry ditch, sticking out forward of the redoubt, is a *capponière* – a strong covered way from which defenders can fire laterally, along the bottom of the moat. Above is the gun platform for four guns, probably twenty-four-pounders, able to traverse left and right as well as to shoot straight ahead. There were also guns on top of the barrack block covering the approach road from the west. The whole was a formidable obstacle to anyone intending to march on Dublin from Galway and it is with a certain guilty sorrow that it has to be recognised that, because it was never disputed in war, there is no story to tell of daring deeds done here.

The construction of these mighty defence works all along the river would have been useless if they had been kept short of powder, shot and supplies. The improvement of the Shannon navigation had been proposed even earlier than 1697 when a petition to the Irish Parliament estimated that it would be possible to build a canalised system from Carrick to Limerick for £14,000. Some work was authorised in 1715 but serious undertakings began with the Meelick works in 1755. They reached Athlone in 1757 and had gone on to Carrick in the 1780s. The Grand Canal from Dublin was completed to Shannon Harbour, downstream of Shannonbridge, in 1804. A military barracks was built and by 1806 2,000 troops could be housed with room for half as many again in times of emergency. It is interesting to note that the first modern canal in England, the Bridgewater, was not started until 1759. In 1805 the Blisworth tunnel on the Grand Union Canal in Northamptonshire was opened and the inland water route between Liverpool and London was complete. It thus became possible to transport supplies and men from London to the Shannon by water. Cannon balls and gunpowder are heavy and poorly suited to transportation by road. The development of the canal system was central to the effectiveness of military defences against invaders at the dawn of the nineteenth century.

No invaders came. The conflict which later troubled Ireland was a colonial war or a war of independence or suppression of a rebellion depending on where one stood at the time. Just one event, the Castleconnel Incident, as narrated by Charles Townshend, illustrates the desperate and disgraceful level to which matters had sunk by 1921.

Castleconnel lies on the Shannon just a few miles north east of Limerick. On 19 April, G Company of the Auxiliary Division, Royal Irish Constabulary made a raid on the Shannon Hotel to search for suspects, members of the IRA (the Volunteers). The Company was divided into two detachments, one in plain clothes and the other in uniform. Two officers and twelve cadets were supposed to go into the hotel without attracting attention while their uniformed comrades, armed with two Lewis guns – light .303 machine-guns – as well as rifles and revolvers and commanded by another officer surrounded the place ready to capture quarry flushed out of cover. As they drove up they saw men running away. It excited them immensely but their reaction was anything but rational. The plain-clothes men rushed into the bar and bellowed, 'Hands up!' It happened that three Royal Irish Constabulary officers were having

The tête-de-pont at Shannonbridge, possibly the finest example of its kind in Europe. The glacis runs from the lower right, out of the picture, up to a dry stone-faced ditch in front of the main gun platform.

themselves an off-duty drink there, and thinking they were the objects of attack, drew their guns and opened fire. The Auxiliaries were driven out into the courtyard where one of them, Donald Pringle, was killed and one of the three men remaining in the bar died also, an RIC sergeant, William Hughes. At this point the uniformed Auxiliaries rolled up and it became evident to the men in the hotel that they were fighting their own side, so they attempted to surrender.

At this point the story diverges. The official version has it that the Auxiliaries were slow to cease fire and that one RIC man and the landlord, Denis O'Donovan, were hit. O'Donovan died of three gunshot wounds to his front, one in the side and two in his back. All very unfortunate. But inconveniently for the officials, a surgeon of some distinction, Mr Cripps, was in the hotel and saw things very differently. The Auxiliaries, he said, ran amok, continuing to fire and rampaging about, quite out of control. Mr Cripps had a brother who happened to be Lord Parmoor, a man destined to serve in the British Labour Government and to sire a future member of government, Sir Stafford Cripps. Parmoor read out his brother's account of the affair in the House of Lords and demanded a full inquiry. He was told that one was already in progress, the Military Court of Inquiry in Lieu of Inquest. And when that reported the whole of Cripps's testimony was brushed aside with the suggestion that he had been confused by the unusual experience of witnessing gunfire. As happens so often under all governments, inconvenient news is no news.

5

The Far North West

Battle of **Farsetmore** ✕ Derry

Donegal

Ford of the Biscuits
• Sligo • Enniskillen
• Killala

• Castlebar   Ballinamuck

Dublin •

The extreme north west of Ireland, Donegal, lacks features attractive to an aggressor. It is plentifully supplied with mountains and narrow passes and only in the north, on either side of the ancient O'Neill stronghold of the Inishowen peninsula, is there a promise of entry. Here, to the west, Lough Swilly and, to the east, Lough Foyle, cut deep into the land to the towns of Letterkenny and Derry, or Londonderry, respectively. South west of Donegal is the great sweep of Donegal Bay, at first glance a tempting landing place. Do not be misled. If the north east, Ulster, is the objective the way is barred by two great bodies of water, the upper and lower parts of Lough

Grianan of Aileach, the restored ancient O'Neill stronghold, overlooks Lough Swilly.

Erne, between which sits the strategically important and well-fortified site of Enniskillen and south of there a straggle of loughs restricts movement and channels forces into predictable locations. The southern edge of Donegal Bay has two lesser bays cut into it. At Sligo a brief hinterland separates the sea from Loughs Allen and Arrow and the numerous small bodies of water around the headwaters of the Shannon. Further west Killala Bay gives onto a north-facing cup of uplands cradling Lough Conn. No matter which way an attacker comes at this country, he is likely to lose against defenders familiar with the mountains and loughs.

Magh Tuireadh, A Mythical Battle

Of all the ancient battles described in the myths of Ireland only one, Magh Tuireadh, appears to have a location agreed by a fair number of people. Exactly where it took place cannot be said, but the Plain of Weeping or the Plain of Towers, as it has been rendered, is claimed to be Moytura, near Lough Arrow. There were, in the stories, two battles of the same name. Both involved on the one side the people who called themselves the Tuatha Dé Danann, the People of the Goddess Danu or Anu. The first of their fights was against the Firbolgs, but that is said to have taken place near Cong in County Mayo. The defeated Firbolgs then fled to the Aran Islands and built stone forts. The second happened near Lough Arrow and was against the Fomorians, a Scandinavian tribe of sea-raiders with their base on Tory Island, off the Donegal coast. They had, it appears, come to dominate the Dé Danann and the fight was to break free of their oppression.

The leader of the Tuatha Dé Danann was a demi-god called Lugh, meaning Light, a person of great beauty and every known skill. His companions decided to keep him out of the battle lest they lose him. Before they fought Lugh quizzed his men of rank and ascertained their particularly useful abilities in war: the making of spears, shields, weapon shafts, the ability to fight and win over many men and – this was on the part of the sorcerers – the power to prevent the enemy from urinating. Apparently this would deplete their strength. Chief amongst the Fomorians was Balor, son of Dot son of Nét, a person of very peculiar talents, as will appear.

So they came to battle, but Lugh had evaded the attention of the man set to guard him and led his people in attack. He also exhorted them to courage in the protection of their country and cast a beneficial spell upon them, dancing round them on one leg and with one eye closed. Then battle was joined, and many fell in the conflict. A translation of a sixteenth-century manuscript of Giolla Riabhach Ó Cléirigh says:

> As they hacked at each other their fingertips and their feet almost met; and because of the slipperiness of the blood under the warriors' feet, they kept falling down, and their heads were cut off as they sat. A gory, wound-inflicting, sharp, bloody battle was upheaved, and spearshafts were reddened in the hands of foes.

Then Lugh and Balor met and the Fomorian made ready to use his eye. It was an eye of particular power, able to render any and all who saw it unable to fight. It was never opened, save in battle, and had to be exposed by lifting a ring fastened in the eyelid. Balor called upon his companions to lift the eyelid, and as they did so Lugh released a

One of the Nymphsfield prehistoric stone circles near the alleged site of the first Battle of Moytura.

Tory Island, off the Donegal coast, the Fomorian stronghold. The trenchworks that protected the promontory fort, Balor's Fort, can be seen across the narrowest part of the near peninsula.

The possible site of the second Battle of Moytura, in the parish of Kilmactranny, north-east of Lough Arrow.

stone from his slingshot with such power that, when it struck the eye, it forced it clean back through Balor's head to gaze upon his own men and as the warrior fell he crushed twenty-seven of his own side beneath him. With that the Fomorians broke and the Tuatha Dé Danann were victorious.

O'Neill and the Gallowglass

Conn O'Neill had been an ally of Gearóid Óg FitzGerald, the ninth Earl of Kildare, but was forced to come to an agreement with Henry VIII and in 1542 accept the regrant of his earldom, though not that of Ulster, with the title of Tyrone. He designated his illegitimate, adopted son, Matthew, Baron Dungannon, as his heir. His actual son, Shane, took this amiss, slew Matthew in 1558 and relegated his father to exile in which he died the following year. This did not increase the confidence of an Elizabethan court attempting to stabilise English power in Ireland at a time when the Spanish were endangering the kingdom, especially as Shane's claim to the chieftainship was based on election by the clan rather than English law. A negotiated settlement was made when Shane O'Neill visited England and made formal submission to Elizabeth, but on his return to Ireland he pursued his efforts to best the O'Donnells of Tyrconnell and the Scots-related clan of the MacDonalds. Within his own family Shane's nephew, Hugh O'Neill, was obliged to seek sanctuary amongst the English of the Pale while his uncle remained alive.

Harry Avery's Castle, built by Henry Aimbreidh O'Neill, who died in 1392. This Irish castle near Newtownstewart dominated the approach to the O'Neill lands by the route through Omagh and Strabane.

The Scots of Antrim were intimately connected with their cousins in Scotland and could call on them in time of trouble. Sir Henry Bagenal of Newry wrote in 1586, '...they are supplied as need requireth from Scotland ... by making of fires upon certain steep rocks hanging over the sea.' Incoming Scots were employed as mercenaries as the gallowglass, now resident in Ireland, had been in the past. Their system of employment was called *buannacht*, a three-month contract that billeted them on civilians. The soldiers thus became known as bonnaghts. The Scots were also known as redshanks because they wore kilts and were bare-legged below. Elizabeth regarded the Antrim Scots as enemies and approved of Shane O'Neill's actions against them while it suited her. He beat the MacDonalds at Ballycastle in north-east Antrim on 2 May 1564 in what became known as the Battle of Glenshesk, killing more than 700 of them by his own count. Elizabeth's response was to befriend the survivors and encourage them to oppose O'Neill.

The Battle of Glenshesk was fought in the open field, a contrast to the tactics Shane O'Neill had used in opposing the government forces sent against him by the earl of Sussex in 1560, 1561 and 1563. Then he had kept to the woods and employed the traditional ambush to harass his enemies when he was not evading contact altogether. He had also recruited men from the lowest level of society, the unfree tillers of the land. Traditionally the fighters were drawn only from the freemen, both here and in Scotland, but Shane trained ploughmen and the like to military service, and thus his forces included freemen, gallowglass and these peasants whom no one knew personally. It was

Letterkenny in the distance beyond the difficult waters of Lough Swilly in which the O'Neill men were trapped after the Battle of Farsetmore.

this mixing of men that was to be Shane's weak point, for it meant that spies could circulate within his camp unsuspected.

Shane O'Neill had managed to make confirmed enemies of the O'Donnells of Tyrconnell. He had defeated Calvagh O'Donnell, his father-in-law, in 1559, hauled the man around in manacles as a prisoner, much to the grief of his, Shane's, wife, and compounded the insult by taking his mother-in-law to his bed and begetting bastards on her. Calvagh was released in 1564 and sought relief from the Lord Deputy, Sir Henry Sidney. In 1566 Elizabeth had had enough of Shane and Sidney made the first move by restoring Calvagh to his chieftainship, in which he was to die within a month to be succeeded by his brother, Hugh O'Donnell, Shane O'Neill's nephew. The English undertook a campaign against Shane O'Neill, putting a force in at the south of Lough Foyle at a place called Derry and sending an army north from the Pale to secure Hugh O'Donnell's position. Edward Randolph, Lieutenant of the Ordnance, led the Derry force and entrenched the place ready to oppose Shane O'Neill. In September 1566 Sidney arrived, installed Hugh O'Donnell, and left. As soon as he was gone O'Neill besieged Derry but was beaten off, although Randolph was killed in the fighting. Next spring, in April, the garrison's gunpowder blew up, killing many of them and leaving them defenceless, so the English withdrew from Derry. Shane O'Neill now seized the opportunity to attack Hugh O'Donnell.

O'Donnell was at a small fort at Ardingary, near to Letterkenny and to the north east of

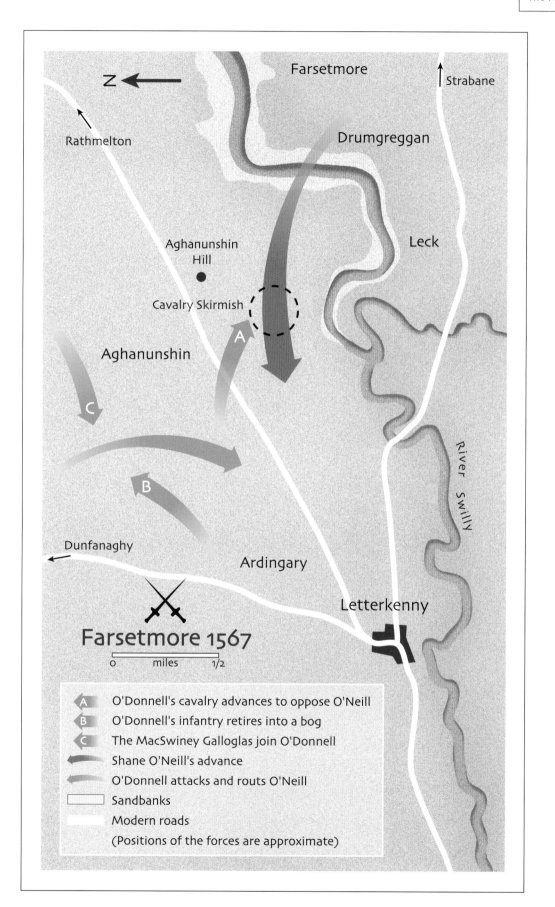

Z ←

Farsetmore

↑ Strabane

↑ Rathmelton

Drumgreggan

Leck

Aghanunshin
Hill
●

Cavalry Skirmish

A

Aghanunshin

C

B

River Swilly

Dunfanaghy
←

Ardingary

Letterkenny

⚔

Farsetmore 1567

0   miles   1/2

A	O'Donnell's cavalry advances to oppose O'Neill
B	O'Donnell's infantry retires into a bog
C	The MacSwiney Galloglas join O'Donnell
	Shane O'Neill's advance
	O'Donnell attacks and routs O'Neill
	Sandbanks
	Modern roads

(Positions of the forces are approximate)

A tomb at Dungiven Priory, County Derry. The prone figure is of Cumhadh na nGall Ó Catháin, who died in 1385, but the panel below, depicting gallowglass, is of a later date.

it at the southern end of Lough Swilly. When he became aware of Shane's approach he sent for more of his men, but by dawn on 8 May they had not yet arrived. Shane O'Neill's army marched towards the ford across the River Swilly at Farsetmore or Fearsad Suilighe, downstream, that is east, of O'Donnell's position. The tide was out and they had no difficulty in crossing. Hugh O'Donnell sent his son with the horse to delay the enemy and led his small band of foot-soldiers north into a bog where they would be hard to get at. The cavalry would have been light and armed with spears, mounted on pads rather than full saddles and without stirrups, so they were capable of thrusting with or throwing their spears but could not charge with them couched like lances. The young man, also called Hugh, led his men well, causing significant damage to Shane O'Neill's men and then pulling back to rejoin his father. Then the gallowglass began to arrive. First was Murrough MacSwiney, then came the boys of the MacSwiney Fanad and finally Maolmuire Mac Swiney Baghaineach. The numbers of the gallowglass are not known. The storytellers were partial to their side and so minimised their strength to increase their glory; they say four hundred.

Meanwhile Shane O'Neill had taken over the position at Ardingary and was making camp with a view to making it a base from which to plunder and destroy the Tirconnell domains. Wasting no time, Hugh O'Donnell gathered his force and attacked. There must have been enough time during his approach for O'Neill to organise his troops, and they seem to have met their attackers in reasonably good order, for the fighting went on for a long time. The chroniclers are unhelpful, for there is a great deal about blood, courage and mayhem and nothing at all about what actually took place in military terms. Eventually Shane O'Neill's men withdrew towards the ford over which they had come, but the tide had come in. The sandbank over which they had crossed with such ease was now deep under water. Many of the beaten force were drowned, but it is hard to determine the true number. Sir Henry Sidney reported to Queen Elizabeth that 613 were found dead, but where they were found we do not know. Perhaps on dry land, before the drowning started. Some tale-tellers say 1,300 and yet others say 3,000. In any case, it was no trivial thing.

Shane O'Neill got away. He went upstream to a ford near Scarriffhollis, two miles west of Letterkenny, and made for Tyrone. It is doubtful that he was in his right mind. The annalists say his reason was disturbed and his behaviour supports that. Of all people he appealed for help to Alexander Óg MacDonald, the brother of James who had died of wounds after Shane's victory at the Battle of Glenshesk. Shane rode with fifty horsemen to Cushendun on the eastern coast of Antrim and there he and his host were generously entertained with food and drink. Perhaps a little too much drink, for they fell to quarrelling and Alexander's men slaughtered Shane and his followers, cut off Shane's head, pickled it and sent it to Dublin where it was displayed on a spike at the castle. The error of fighting with a river at your back was clearly demonstrated and it is interesting to speculate about Shane's successor to the earldom, his brother's son Hugh, and what he might have been thinking at Kinsale thirty-four years later when he faced the English with a river at their back.

The Pass of Enniskillen

After Shane's death in 1567 Toirdhealbhach (Turlough) Luineach O'Neill became the

*Lower Lough Erne, a beautiful barrier to military movement which, together with the Upper Lough
and numerous other lakes, gives Enniskillen its strategic importance.*

O'Neill and reinforced his position by marriage, two years later, to Agnes Campbell. This
gave him a ready supply of warriors from Scotland, and more power than the English
cared to see. Hugh O'Neill became the answer to the English problem until he, too,
became strong and then an attempt was made to support Turlough against him. The
English had been creeping forward in the north and north west of Ireland, building
forts and garrisoning towns, but Hugh O'Neill at first avoided direct confrontation. He
made an ally of his family's traditional enemies, the O'Donnells, by giving his daughter
in marriage to Red Hugh O'Donnell (Aodh Ruadh Ó Domhnaill). In fact the transaction
did not proceed smoothly, for the Lord Deputy, Sir John Perrott, was not at all in favour
of it and had Red Hugh kidnapped and locked up in Dublin Castle for four years. With
his future father-in-law's help he eventually escaped and when he got home in 1592 his
mother had his senile father displaced so he became lord of Tirconnell. Perrott had
succeeded unwittingly in engineering a solid anti-English power bloc in the north west
that would endure until the two great leaders were defeated at Kinsale.

The President of Connaught, Sir Richard Bingham, had been trying to extend English
influence in north Connacht and Ulster and had taken the century-old Maguire castle at
Enniskillen in 1594. An illustration of the time shows both cannon fire and musketry
being brought to bear on the castle, and a breach made in a curtain wall. Three ships are
shown, at first standing off and ready for action and then in use alongside the castle on
its island. One, well-covered with a protective roof, conveyed sixty-seven men to exploit
the breach while the other two were equipped with scaling ladders and carried thirty men
to use them. Enniskillen was a key location, for the only routes into or out of western
Ulster were, as they are today, along the coast at Ballyshannon and up towards Strabane

Ballinafad Castle guarding the pass in the Curlew Mountains, site of the battle of 1599.

or between the two loughs at Enniskillen. This route gives access to Omagh or to Dungannon and, with a deviation by way of Newtownbutler, to Monaghan and Armagh. In short, possession of Enniskillen would lock up movement into a significant proportion of the more northerly lands. The English position there was immediately challenged and a relief column was sent to raise the siege.

On 7 August 1594 Cormac MacBaron O'Neill and Hugh Maguire, who was presumably attempting to regain his family's castle, put the English to flight near the River Arney and they lost their supply train when fording the river. All fell into Irish hands, giving the battle the name of Ford of the Biscuits. Hugh O'Neill denied any hand in the matter, but still turned up a couple of days after for his share of the spoils.

Five years later, south west of here, another through-route provided the site of another fight against Queen Elizabeth's power. The principal road from Dublin to Sligo, where both of the routes northwards – coastal and by Enniskillen – converge to avoid the difficult country by the headwaters of the Shannon, passes through Boyle, west of Carrick, before climbing the Curlew Mountains towards Ballinafad. It was here, in 1599, that Red Hugh O'Donnell defeated Sir Conyers Clifford and killed him.

After the defeat at Kinsale the power of the Irish rulers declined until, on 4 September 1607, the Flight of the Earls took place: the O'Neill earl of Tyrone, the O'Donnell earl of Tyrconnell and the Maguire lord of Fermanagh and their followers quit Ireland. They had been plotting with the Spanish to revive their fortunes and perhaps thought they had been found out. In any case, they left a vacuum in that their lands and holdings were forfeit.

Maurice Harron's statue The Gaelic Chieftain *commemorates the Battle of the Curlews.*

Enniskillen Castle originally stood on an island, but today a full appreciation of the terrain is made harder by the changes in water levels modern works have caused.

In 1609 a massive programme of colonisation was approved by King James I. Grants of land of various sizes were made, each carrying with it conditions for defence and settlement. If English and Scots were brought in, rentals were lower than if an all-Irish tenancy prevailed. Enniskillen was to become a new town. Sir Josias Bodley had been appointed to oversee fortifications in Ireland in 1607 and in September of the following year had reported that the former Maguire castle was 'broken'. By 1611 the new Constable, Captain William Cole, had erected 'a fair and strong wall' which was twenty-six feet high with flankers, that is gun emplacement capable of firing across the face of the wall, and a parapet and wall walk above. The government gave a grant of £200 towards the work. The new town was incorporated in 1613. Sometime after this the Watergate was built, a Scottish-style structure with conical-roofed towers demonstrating, as frequently seen elsewhere in Ulster, the homeland influences of the settlers. A particularly good example is the ruinous Monea Castle, a little to the north west of Enniskillen, completed by Malcolm Hamilton in 1618. The tower-house is rectangular with twin towers at one end which change to a square shape as they rise up. It stands in a bawn, or walled enclosure, which was being built in 1622. It has two circular flankers: corner towers from which fire could be directed along the walls of the bawn. At Enniskillen, what is now known as Forthill was a grazing area in 1611, where the inhabitants of the new town were given the right to graze their livestock. At that time, before modern works changed the water levels here, Lough Erne flooded to the foot of the hill.

The succession of James II to the throne in 1689 gave the Protestants considerable cause for alarm and the Governor of Enniskillen, Gustavus Hamilton, ordered the fortification of the hill. A sconce – a fort of earth sods – was made. It was a rectangular structure with bastions at each corner, the footprint of which can be traced around the mid-nineteenth century Cole Monument in the park that now crowns Forthill. It was connected to the town and castle by a covered way, long since removed. James had landed at Kinsale on 12 March and by early summer operations were in hand to bring Ulster under his control, principally the centres of Londonderry and Enniskillen. In fact Upper and Lower Lough Erne, Ballyshannon and Enniskillen formed a considerable threat to the Jacobite route to Londonderry and all this line was in Protestant hands, that is, the supporters of King William III. There had been an attempt by Viscount Galmoy to oust them in March, but they had seen him off without too much difficulty. Indeed, Hamilton and Thomas Lloyd took the fight to the Jacobites by launching raids to within forty miles of Dublin. Patrick Sarsfield and Lieutenant-General Conrad von Rosen both led forays to deal with these raiders, and a more substantial effort against Enniskillen commanded by the Duke of Berwick was prevented from taking the town and castle because it was ordered away to Londonderry to prevent that town's relief.

In July Justin MacCarthy, Viscount Mountcashel, led three regiments of foot, sixteen troops of cavalry and eight field guns to roll up the Lough Erne line. He joined forces with Major-General Anthony Hamilton with his dragoons and Cuconnacht Mór Maguire and his Ulster Gaels. From the relief force outside Londonderry Major-General Piercy Kirke sent Colonel William Wolseley by sea to Enniskillen with supplies. On 30 July Mountcashel began his campaign by advancing from Clones, to the east, and attacking Crom Castle on the eastern shore of Upper Lough Erne, near Newtownbutler. To the aid of Crom came Lieutenant-Colonel William Berry who was then attacked by Hamilton's dragoons and fell back towards Newtownbutler, leading his enemies into an ambush, an Irish tactic that should have been recognised. Wolseley then arrived to back up Berry against Mountcashel's force of some 4,000 men south of the town. The Jacobite position was on rising ground with a bog before it across which there was a causeway that was covered by a gun emplacement. The infantry from Enniskillen swarmed across the bog and slaughtered the gunners, to be followed by the cavalry across the now undefended causeway. Meanwhile, perhaps because of a wrong or misunderstood order, Hamilton's dragoons withdrew with their commander leading the way. Mountcashel's remaining men were quickly surrounded and those slow to surrender were killed. The Jacobite losses were numbered at 1,000 dead and 500 made prisoner. Of those who managed to get away, many drowned in the lough. It was a substantial victory for the Williamites and meant that the besieging force at Londonderry could not look to James for further reinforcement. The front stabilised with the Williamites in possession of the line from Ballyshannon south-eastwards while, although the town changed hands more than once, the Jacobites held Sligo.

An outpost at *Doire*, the place of the oaks, or Derry, was the purpose of Sir Henry Docwra when he founded the new fortification in 1600 to create an inroad into the territory of the O'Neill. In 1613 a charter was granted to London companies for the settlement of the area and the name of the town was changed to Londonderry, though the name related to the old Irish is favoured by those to whom the reference to the capital city of Great Britain is a source of annoyance. The stone walls were finished in

Monea Castle, built in 1618 by Malcolm Hamilton, within a bawn added in 1622. It is a fine example of a planter tower house.

Crom Castle, on the shores of Upper Lough Erne.

Roaring Meg, a cannon dating from 1642, on the walls of Derry high above the Bogside.

1618, making it the last walled town to be built in western Europe. When it was approached by the Jacobite army in April 1689, the Williamite governor, Robert Lundy, was inclined to surrender, but the citizens would have none of that and Major Henry Baker and the Reverend George Walker assumed the command. The ramparts and bastions were strengthened with a ravelin – a detached triangular fortification – outside Bishop's Gate and redoubts and trenches were constructed on Windmill Hill.

The siege began on 18 April, with the population of 2,000 added to with 30,000 refugees and 7,000 soldiers. The Jacobites lacked the firepower to deal with the massive walls and although assaults took place the strategy was essentially one of starving the Williamites out. A boom was made across the river to prevent relief by water-borne forces. A relief force under Major-General Piercy Kirke was sent but was slow to come into action and the starving inhabitants of the town were paying as much as six pence for a mouse. At the end of July two ships, the *Mountjoy* and the *Phoenix*, made the attempt to break the boom. Writing nearly a century later, the Chevalier de Latocnaye expressed surprise that the boom had been vulnerable as it evidently protected the only route through which supplies could come to the beleaguered town. He said, with what precise accuracy it is hard to know,

> The frigate, carried by a good breeze and by the tide current, struck the boom with violence, and by the rebound was thrown so far out of the channel as to be stranded; but, happily, the captain, profiting by the rising tide, freed his ship by the expedient of firing the whole of the cannons on the side on which the vessel had touched ground, and the tide carried the ship through the boom, which had been broken by the first shock. When the frigate had passed through, the captain and crew cried 'Huzza! huzza!' (called here three cheers), and had the misfortune in commencing the third 'huzza' to have his head carried off by a cannon ball.

The rescuing ships reached the town that evening, 28 July. The Jacobites abandoned the siege. It is said that some 15,000 people, mainly women and children, had died of starvation or disease in the 105 days they had been confined to that place.

The Year of the French

The greatest puzzle, as what was optimistically called the Year of Liberty, 1798, rolled forward, was where were the French? There had been uprisings of the United Irishmen in Wexford, in Ulster and other places, and it was now understood by the new Lord

Killala, County Mayo, the first town to fall to the French in 1798.

Lieutenant, Charles Cornwallis, that the objective had been the establishment of a republic. If that was the case why had the French not invaded as they had attempted to do at Bantry Bay? By the middle of August it appeared that the risings were over at the cost of about 25,000 lives, of which 2,000 or so had been loyalists. If we assume something of the order of ten per cent fatalities, the numbers of combatants had been huge. On 20 August intelligence was received of the presence of six frigates and a ship of the line, the *Hoche*, in Brest, ready to sail with 3,800 soldiers. No news of their evading the Royal Navy's blockade had come, but precautions were taken against a landing in the south or in the west.

In the event the landing took place at Killala, in the centre of the southern shore of Donegal Bay. Here, on 23 August, the French arrived, some 1,099 men under General Jean Humbert. It was announced:

> ... behold Frenchmen arrived amongst you ... The moment of breaking your chains is arrived ... Can there be any Irishman base enough to separate himself at such a happy conjuncture from the grand interests of his country? If there be, brave friends, let him be chased from the Country he betrays and let his property become the reward of those generous men who knew how to fight and die ... Union! Liberty! the Irish Republic! ... Let us march ...

Stirring stuff if you could read the proclamation and understand what it meant. Cornwallis received the news calmly and prepared to move against the invaders, working on the assumption that they were just the first of a much larger force, and in this he was correct. Humbert's ships had come from La Rochelle and the 3,000 or so troops in Brest under General Hardy were due to arrive together with another 4,000 from Dunkirk. Wolfe Tone would be with the Brest contingent. At least Napoleon himself would not be joining them. The *London Gazette* of 30 August reported:

> *Thursday, August 30.* Information respecting Bounaparte, and the expedition under his command, has been received; to which, we believe, a very small degree of doubt can attach. From accounts that are considered as official we learn, that at least a principal part, if not the whole of the French fleet, has arrived in safety at Alexandria.

So the Egypt Expedition was gone to the far end of the Mediterranean and was therefore safely out of the way. On the events on Ireland the same issue carried the following from the Duke of Portland:

> *Whitehall, August 30.* My Lord, I have the satisfaction to acquaint your Lordship, that dispatches have been received at Dublin-Castle, from Major-Gen. [Francis] Hutchinson, dated Castlebar, the 25th instant, which states that the French troops who disembarked at Killala had not attempted to march into the country, nor had they been joined by any number of the inhabitants; and that the Major-General was proceeding to act against the enemy with the King's troops, who were receiving every assistance from the people of the country. Before the arrival of the Major-General's dispatches, the Lord Lieutenant had left Dublin, and proceeded to take command of the army.

Humbert was obeying orders while Hutchinson was not. Cornwallis had directed his subordinates to avoid contact with the French unless they had overwhelming superiority and could be sure of victory. Humbert had been told to wait for Hardy and, when the senior man was located, place himself under his orders. In the meantime his task was to recruit locally and Matthew Tone, brother of Theobald Wolfe Tone, was there to help. In Brest, things were not going well. The ships were ready, the men were present, but their pay was not. It took two weeks for the money to arrive and then, when at last they went to sea, two frigates collided as they attempted to break through the British blockade; the Royal Navy had forty-two ships off Brest. The French turned back. On 26 August orders arrived to delay the attempt until the autumn gales had scattered the British blockade. The Dunkirk contingent, the largest, was not to go at all. The French commitment to the Irish enterprise was anything but absolute.

In Killala the French went about inducting the Irish into the army. Helmets and uniforms were issued and arms handed out. As this went on they became dismayed by the quality of men joining up, for they had no knowledge of firearms and seemed more interested in having new clothes than in any military topic. Supplies were purchased with drafts drawn on a non-existant Directory of Connacht and, on 25 August, leaving a couple of hundred men and a colonel behind to secure the place, the French left Killala for Ballina, the next town to the south. A brief skirmish outside the town put the yeomanry in retreat and Ballina was abandoned to the enemy, the British retiring to Foxford, east of the other end of Lough Conn.

General Hutchinson had now received an explicit instruction from Cornwallis not to attack with his small force. He therefore set up a garrison to hold Foxford and created a position north west of Castlebar for his remaining 1,700 troops, his ten curricle guns – small weapons mounted on wheels similar to those of the light, two-wheeled, two-horse carriage of the same name – and his howitzer. At eleven o'clock at night on Sunday, 26 August, Lieutenant-General Gerard Lake arrived to assume command. At about three o'clock the next morning a farmer came in to report a column of men in blue uniforms and at five General Trench went out to see. He returned in some haste after coming under musket fire.

Humbert had not, as expected, taken the road to Foxford to participate in an encounter with the waiting garrison. Reconnaissance had shown that there was an alternative, a slender, mountainous route west of Lough Conn. The French marched on the afternoon of 26 August and came on steadily to arrive outside Castlebar at six in the morning. The position taken by the British is described by Thomas Pakenham.

> Castlebar lay in a hollow, beside a small river flowing from the mountainous country to the north-west; low hills protected it on either side. On one of these, called Sion Hill, the front line had been established: four curricle guns ... two manned by experienced gunners, and several hundred musketeers ... Behind them was a second line of musketeers ...

Then there was a third line and cavalry in reserve. As the French advanced Lake ordered

Ballina, on the River Moy, commanding the route south from Killala.

his artillery to open fire. The attackers, without artillery, were unable to reply but advanced doggedly. Colonel Sarrazin led his Grenadiers along a ditch that gave some cover, but still men were falling like nine-pins. The Irish troops on the French side had fled. Now the Irish on the other side did the same, leaving the guns and the Fencibles isolated. The Grenadiers, with the bayonet, got in amongst the few brave enough to stand. The commanders tried to rally their men, but it was useless. The sight of the battle-hardened French troops coming relentlessly on behind cold steel was too much for them. They ran. All the guns and all the supplies fell into French hands. The event went down in history as the Castlebar Races.

The material and manpower losses were not great. Fifty-three men had been killed, thirty-six wounded and two hundred and seventy-eight were 'missing', some few joining the French but the rest just slipping away or taking up plundering and banditry in the disordered countryside. Nine cannon had been lost to the French. What was more serious was the credibility it gave to a renewed insurrection and many feared that Meath and Kildare would once more be up in arms. In the north west the military situation was much more secure. Humbert could not do anything of significance to the west of Castlebar, for there was nothing important there. No serious route south existed through Connemara into western Galway and the eastern route was seriously exposed to the bulk of the British strength coming from Dublin by canal to Tullamore and thence to Athlone, while General Hewett had brought men from the south to Portumna on the Shannon at the northern end of Lough Derg. The Shannon had also to be crossed to evade such a force by the north and any attempt to enter Ulster would run into the Lough Erne line as in earlier wars. General George Nugent had moved to Enniskillen. Humbert was fairly effectively trapped and unless reinforcements arrived his defeat was just a matter of time and stolid, sensible generalship by Cornwallis. The danger of Humbert's being reinforced was countered by assiduous patrolling by the Royal Navy.

In London there was deep concern, but no panic. Reinforcements were hurried to Ireland. Cornwallis pushed 7,800 men up to Tuam, halfway between Athlone and Castlebar, by 2 September, covering any possible attempt by Humbert to head for Galway town. General Taylor and 2,800 men were in Boyle, just west of Carrick-on-Shannon. Two days later the British moved from Tuam, their numbers now augmented to 10,000, closer to Castlebar with the intention of attacking the following day.

Humbert, in the meanwhile, had been attempting to create a form of civil power with a dozen men constituting a council of provisional government and a declaration being made that all men between sixteen and forty years of age were required to enlist in the army. The small towns on the coast to the west, Newport and Westport, had risen and some men of rank had come out for the cause. Three quarters of County Mayo was under Humbert's control. However, he had no cash to pay his regulars or his new soldiers and looting was sullying the purity of his force. The French had, indeed, been particular in their respect for people and property, and now Humbert felt obliged to have two Irish captains shot for failure to control their men. However, staying in Castlebar until Cornwallis chose to smash his army was clearly not an option. Nor could he expect reinforcements at an early date. His only hope was to go east and trust that enough Irishmen would join him to make an advance on Dublin practical.

He moved swiftly towards Sligo where the garrison commander, Colonel Vereker, arrayed his small force at Collooney, a town on the road south of Sligo. It was not a mighty encounter, but some fifty men lost their lives and a hundred of the Irish militia and yeomanry were forced to surrender. Humbert sent them back to Sligo on parole. The French continued, but veered slightly east to Dromahair. From there they might make for Enniskillen and Ulster, or perhaps turn south east towards the Shannon and, beyond it, the Midlands. Later, on 8 September, Cornwallis wrote:

> I had every reason to believe, from the enemy's movements to Drumahair, that it was their intention to march to the North; and it was natural to suppose that they might hope that a French force would get into some of the bays in that part of the country, without succour of which kind every point of direction for their march seemed equally desperate. I received, however, very early in the morning of the 7th, accounts from Lieut-Gen. Lake, that they had turned to their right to Drumkeirn [Drumkeeran], and that he had reason to believe that it was their intention to go to Boyle, or Carrick on Shannon; in consequence of which I hastened the march of the troops under my immediate command, in order to arrive before the enemy at Carrick, and directed Major-Gen. [John] Moore who was at Tubercurry, to be prepared, in the event of the enemy's movement to Boyle.

The intelligence that had reached Cornwallis was correct. Hearing of risings in the Midlands, and indeed there was one at Edgeworthstown on 4 September, Humbert had decided to turn south east. He abandoned his captured cannon to make greater speed

North east of Sligo the bulk of the mountains of Truskmore and Ben Bulben reduce the options for movement to clinging to the coast or turning east for Enniskillen. This view is from the north.

and was at Drumkeeran on the evening of 6 September, marching down the western side of Lough Allen the next day to cross the Shannon at Balintra at noon and reach Cloone, twelve miles north of Longford, in the evening. His movements were carefully observed by British cavalry under Colonel Robert Craufurd. Lieutenant-General Lake wrote of him:

> Lieut.-Col. Crauford, who commanded my advanced corps, composed of detachments of Hompesch's and the 1st fencible cavalry, by great vigilance and activity, hung close upon their rear, that they could not escape from me, although they drove the country, and carried with them all the horses.

Cornwallis again:

> On my arrival at Carrick, I found that the enemy had passed the Shannon at Balintra, where they attempted to destroy the bridge; but Lieut.-Gen. Lake followed them so closely, that they were not able to effect it. Under these circumstances I felt pretty confident, that one more march would bring this disagreeable warfare to a conclusion; and, having obtained satisfactory information that the enemy had halted for the night at Cloone, I moved with the troops at Carrick, at 10 o'clock on the night of the 7th, to Mohill [south west of Cloone], and directed Lieut.-Gen. Lake to proceed at the same time to Cloone, which is about three miles from Mohill ...

A cannon, described as a captured French six-pounder, outside the nineteenth-century Royal Irish Constabulary barracks at Ballinamuck. The English reports of the battle speak, however, only of four-pounders being taken.

Humbert's intention was to link with the Midland rebels at Granard, but men from the garrison of Cavan, 250 local yeomanry and 100 Argyll Fencibles under one Major Porter, had already set off to oppose the much greater number of Irish there. The rebels indeed attacked the town, but Porter joined with the local garrison in the defeat and slaughter of the leaderless mob. Something between 400 and 1,000 of them were killed for government casualties of two wounded. From there Porter marched on to deal with the rebels at Wilson's Hospital, on the Longford road outside Mullingar, where their opportunities for retreat had been blocked by militia led down from Castlepollard by Lord Longford. A mere 200 were killed here as it was late in the day and the rest escaped in the dusk. The survivors of the United Irishmen armies of Westmeath and Longford reached Humbert at Cloone on the night of 7 September.

Humbert moved on for Granard on the morning of 8 September with Craufurd directly behind him. Cornwallis had moved to St John's Town, now called Ballinalee, on the road between Longford and Granard to block the way to Dublin. At Ballinamuck the final act was played out. Lake reported:

> [I] arrived at Cloone about 7 o'clock this morning [8 September], where having received directions to follow the enemy on the same line, while his Excellency [Cornwallis] moved by the lower road to intercept them, I advanced, having previously detached the Monaghan light company, mounted behind dragoons, to harrass their rear. Lieut.-Col. Crauford, on coming up with the French rearguard, summoned them to surrender; but as they did not attend to his summons, he attacked them; upon which upwards of 200 French infantry threw down their arms, under the idea that the rest of the corps would do the same thing; and Capt. Pakenham, Lieut.-Gen. of Ordnance, and Major-Gen. Craddock, rode up to them. The enemy, however, instantly commenced a fire of cannon and musketry, which wounded Gen. Craddock; upon which I ordered up the third battalion of light infantry, under the command of Lieut.-Col. Innes, and commenced the attack upon the enemy's position. The action lasted upwards of half an hour, when, the remainder of the column making its appearance, the French surrendered at discretion. The rebels, who fled in all directions, suffered severely ...

The Irish, it is reported, had been encouraged to get away earlier by Pakenham. The *Dublin Evening Post* of 15 September reported him as calling, 'Run away, boys, otherwise you'll all be cut down.' They stood and were cut down. The English casualties were light. One officer, Lieutenant Stephens of the Carabineers, had been wounded, three private soldiers killed, twelve wounded and three missing. Eleven horses had died, one was wounded and another missing. The three light four-pounder cannon and their five attendant wagons had been taken together with twenty-three French officers, including General Humbert, ninety-six under-officers, seventy-eight grenadiers, four hundred and forty fusiliers, thirty-three carabiniers, sixty chasseurs and forty-one gunners; just under nine hundred men. They were civilly treated and, indeed, a dinner was given for the officers when they reached Dublin. Ninety-six rebels were taken, of whom three were officers, the report says. What happened to them does not appear.

The invasion was over, but the action was not yet complete, for there were still French invasion ships at sea. On 27 August, the day Humbert was putting the defenders of

The site of the Croppies' Graves, Ballinamuck.

Castlebar to flight, James Napper Tandy, a United Irishman who had, through his rivalry with Wolfe Tone, split the movement, set sail from Dunkirk as commander of the *Anacréon* with 270 French Grenadiers and – the principal purpose of the voyage – various supplies, guns, ammunition and powder, to support Humbert. The news of the first landings at Killala had stimulated the French to reinstate General Hardy's expedition, though with only 2,800 men, in eight frigates, a schooner and a ship of the line, the *Hoche*, named after the leader of the Bantry Bay enterprise. With Hardy was Theobald Wolfe Tone.

On 16 September Tandy landed at Rutland Island, off the Donegal coast between Dungloe and Aranmore Island. The news he gathered from the postmaster was not at all what he hoped for: Humbert defeated, the Mayo and Midland risings put down. There was a distribution of republican cockades and hearty, insurrectionist proclamations. The French expressed their willingness to stand by him, but Tandy wisely decided to dine and drink with his friend the postmaster and take his leave. On 17 September the *Anacréon* sailed.

Joseph Stock, Bishop of Killala, had, with his family and other loyalists, been in captivity in his own town all the while, guarded by the small French detachment Humbert had left behind and an increasingly restive company of Irish under the command of Ferdy O'Donnell. No one seemed to know they were still there until a mission was sent to General Trench at Castlebar to extract an assurance that prisoners in his hands would be well treated in return for the mercy granted to the loyalists in Killala. On 23 September Trench appeared outside Killala and the Irish drew up to oppose them. It was no contest. Perhaps some 500 Irish died and maybe a handful of Trench's militia, dragoons and fencibles. The damage and carnage that followed in the town outdid anything the rebels had achieved, loyalist and rebel alike finding themselves grist to the rampaging troops' murderous, thieving mill.

The threat of the second invasion force persisted. On 24 September Sir John Warren sailed with a fleet of six ships to cover the Western Approaches, and four more ships were due to join him. Lord Bridport's fleet had sealed off Brest. On 12 October Warren found the French off the north coast of Donegal and a ten-hour battle ensued. The *Hoche* was taken, with Wolfe Tone aboard, and so were most of the rest of the enemy vessels. Some managed to evade the British as a report in the *Gentleman's Magazine* of November 1798 bears witness.

The Battle of Ballinamuck is commemorated by a statue of an Irish pikeman.

> *Donnegal, October 15.* We were a good deal surprised, on Saturday morning at daybreak, to perceive a French frigate of 30 guns at anchor close-in with the town, and two more in the Bay, all crowded with men. Our drums were set going, and in a few moments we were on the march; however, we could do nothing more than line the coast, as we had no cannon. They sent out 2 boats with about 100 men, just as we got there; but, perceiving us, they returned. The ships remained until yesterday, then departed ... I never knew any thing equal to the loyalty of the country people. After driving away their cattle, and breaking their boats, they armed themselves with pitchforks, and any other weapons they could get, and came down in hundreds along the shore; and I am convinced they would have protected it, even had the militia been away.

Theobald Wolfe Tone entered Dublin in French uniform, a prisoner in irons, on 8 November. At his trial two days later he entered a plea of guilty, speaking with dignity and calm, stating that he had acted on principle alone and asking for a soldier's death before a firing squad. This was denied. In a curious legal move a motion was presented to the Lord Chief Justice which cast doubt on the proceedings that had led to the death sentence, but before the matter could be resolved news arrived that Tone had been found with his throat cut in an attempt at suicide. The poor man had not succeeded; it took him a week to die.

6

The Mountains of Ulster

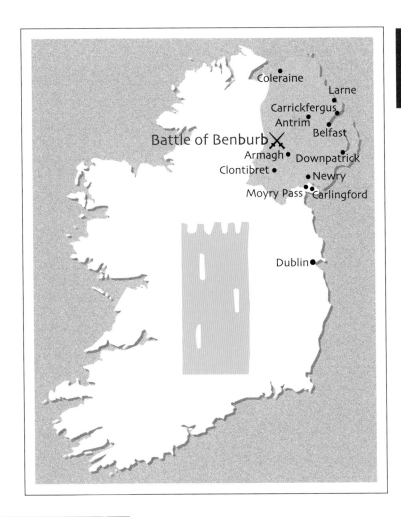

T he north east of Ireland is gathered around the great lake of Lough Neagh from which the Lower Bann flows north and into which the Upper Bann comes from the south east. From the south west the River Blackwater also feeds into the lough with the Sperrin Mountains rising to the west. South east of the Blackwater, behind Armagh, the hills rise to restrict movement, cut only by the narrow valley to Newry and Carlingford Lough, leading to the sea. South from Newry the yet narrower thoroughfare of the Moyry Pass offers access to Dundalk, Drogheda and Dublin. East of Lough Neagh the Antrim Mountains dominate the coast

Narrow Water Castle, a simple tower house within a bawn, guards the confluence of the Newry River with tidal Carlingford Lough, a strategically crucial route into south-eastern Ulster. It was built in the 1650s at a cost of £361 4s 2d.

The ruins of Nendrum Monastery, Mahee Island, Strangford Lough. The site's massive walls proved no defence against Viking raiders and the round tower of about the tenth century may have been built in consequence. John de Courcy founded a Benedictine house here.

down to Belfast Lough, where Carrickfergus Castle protects the sea route to Scotland, and south of Belfast and west of Strangford Lough the land rises again through the hills above Ballynahinch to the Mourne Mountains. It is a land replete with opportunity for small fighting groups and fraught with problems for large bodies of soldiers on the move. It is also very close to Scotland and the sea-orientated chiefdoms of the Western Isles were as ready to regard north-eastern Ireland their land as much as the offshore islands more usually associated with them. Equally, the east-facing loughs proffered a ready welcome to incomers.

The Normans in Ulster

After the arrival of the Normans in the south and then the taking of Dublin, John de Courcy decided to head north. He had arrived in Ireland in 1176 and in Dublin he gathered a force of some 300 men to invade the kingdom of Ulaidh, that is, Ulster, in the following year. Of his background little is known, but he was to found a considerable number of abbeys as his influence grew, and the fact that they were associated with religious houses in Cumbria, England's Lake District, suggests he may have had connections there. The *Book of Howth*, written four hundred years later, is a source for this history and, as it is certainly not contemporary, it must be suspect.

De Courcy's force consisted of twenty-two knights and fifty squires, and foot soldiers made up the rest of his numbers. He made a four-day march to Downpatrick, called Doune in the chronicle, without resistance and the King of the Ulaidh retreated quickly. An attempt was made by a Legate of Rome, one Vivien who came from Scotland, to broker a settlement but de Courcy was not interested, so the King, named here as O'Donyll, gathered his people to attack. It is said 10,000 came and that de Courcy with only 700, presumably because additional men (Welsh archers it can be guessed) had joined his expedition, decided to fight in the open rather than be caught in the town 'like a bird in a cage'. It is clear, however, that he chose his position with care and it would be interesting to locate it today, but the information is very sparse.

De Courcy divided his men into three companies, putting all his horse on his left under the command of his brother, Sir Amorey. There were 140 horse and, with them, 140 archers, although the text often refers to bowmen as merely 'foot', so some confusion can result. Sir Amorey was in a place where the 'ground was but narrow ... toward a great ditch and hedge, where no horseman could come within'. He therefore put his archers behind the hedge. In the centre de Courcy had his men and on his right Roger de Power was close to a marsh. It seems likely that the marsh covered the right flank and the ditch and hedge the left, but it is also said that the approach to Sir Amorey's front was by a narrow place, but what made it narrow – the ground, vegetation or water – is not clear.

The King saw that the horse were few and determined to take them out before setting on his infantry. This seems a sensible decision as he had the advantage of numbers and if the heavily-armed Norman knights could be overcome first the infantry would have nothing to fear from the small remaining Norman army. The Ulaidh attack was with their own horsemen, for the account states that Sir Amorey's reaction was to order his bowmen to reply and 'the shot of arrows came on so fast and their horses were so galled that the horses began to shrink back ...' A distressing image. The Normans charged the Irish cavalry and drove it beyond the narrow pass so that it was separated from their foot, and then called up their own foot to hold the pass and keep the Irish horse there. Turning to his brother, Sir Amorey encouraged him to set his foot on to attack the Irish infantry who were waiting 'in a great trench' for their horse to come up. The fight became a fierce, hand-to-hand contest. As the *Book of Howth* has it:

> There was none that day that Sir John [de Courcy] strack but died with that stroke, beside others that was wounded, but like a wolf amongst a herd of lambs, so did he use himself ... Roger Pouer [de Power] on the right side with his company so well did that there was none that could pass on his side to take succour of the marsh ground ... between him and the main battle there was no way but upon dead corpses, or harness [armour], legs and heads, that lay upon the ground, or such weapons that they had that was slain ...

The Ulaidh then attempted to break out through the thin lines of Sir Amorey's horse, trusting in their nimbleness and lightness of dress to evade the heavily accoutred Normans.

As they came ahead in the plain, [Sir Amorey] met them, running without order,

Clough Castle, south west of Downpatrick, lies on the invasion route of de Courcy and the motte was probably raised by him or one of his followers. The stone keep was raised in about 1200 and the castle seems to have remained in use until about 1500. The great hall was a separate, timber structure.

and set upon them with his horsemen that few stop or could save himself, but that he was able to overrun a horse by speed. There was of this number a two hundred or thereabouts of the Irish, with their leader Rory A'Hanlane [O'Hanlon], that always kept together, and was like to take the plain.

Sir Amorey declared his intention to charge this defiant bunch against the advice of his standard-bearer, Geoffrey Montgomery. When the knight said he would carry his own standard, Montgomery replied, 'Nay, with this standard I hath won my living, and with this standard I will end my life. Now come on, in the name of God and St Patrick.' Sir Amorey was twice unhorsed in the ensuing chase and finally, bleeding freely from a head wound, was surrounded with three of his knights all on foot, using spears seized from the fallen to defend themselves before Sir John's foot came up to rescue him. Meanwhile, the foot left to keep the Irish horse at bay were having a hard time of it.

During this sport [Sir Amorey's chase] few or none escaped; at which time this hundred men, that was left to keep the pass, was inforced to cut the pass, and lay it over with wood, for the horsemen often charged upon them, thinking to come to rescue their fellows that was in the battle ...

They held their barricade of felled trees and, in the opinion of the story-teller, had they

Dundrum Castle, a short way south of Clough, overlooks the west shore of Dundrum Bay. The original ringwork dates from de Courcy's time and was built on the site of an earlier, Irish, defence work. The stone structure was raised by de Courcy before his fall in 1203. The small, square holes around the parapet supported a wooden superstructure.

not done so the King and all his horse would have died with the rest. It sounds as if the pass was a true gulley or narrow valley beyond which the Irish were trapped and that the sides were heavily wooded.

Another action is recounted in which the de Courcy forces were seeking to avenge themselves on O'Hanlon's men after a supply ship had been plundered by them near Newry. It turned out that there were rather more Irish than the Normans cared to tackle, but they resorted to trickery and sent a decoy force to approach from another direction while sending a friar in to the enemy bearing false news of the approach of an additional Norman force. In the event the Irish retreated rather than risk a serious encounter and while doing so half their force became isolated on the far side of the River Larne as the tide came in, permitting the easy slaughter of the remaining part of O'Hanlon's army.

The Norman advance was marked by the construction, first, of mottes and then, in such locations as Carlingford, Greencastle, Dundrum and Carrickfergus, of stone-built castles to provide bases for their domination of the land. Whereas, further south, the Anglo-Irish presence spread far into the interior, their influence in Ulster remained close to the coast in a great arc north and west as far as Lough Foyle. The land they did not take over was that of the Uí Néill.

The Irish Gambit of the Bruce

In 1066 Robert de Bruis left Bruis, near Cherbourg, to invade England with William the Bastard. The expedition was successful and Robert acquired lands in Yorkshire. His son was made Lord of Annandale by David I of Scotland and his descendant married a descendant of David's, Isabel the daughter of the Earl of Huntingdon, who bore a son, Robert le Brus, grandfather of Robert the Bruce and of Edward Bruce. Robert swore fealty to Edward I of England in 1296 but was at war with him a decade later. It was in 1306 that he took refuge on Rathlin Island off the north Antrim coast and legend has it that it was here that he had his encouraging encounter with a spider. In 1307 Edward I died and his feeble son could do little to oppose Robert's steady increase of power and territory culminating in his victory at Bannockburn on 24 June 1314.

The English had not hesitated to use Ireland as a resource to cause the Scots problems. The sea journey across the North Channel was easier to make than to slog over mountains and through bogs as was the norm for land travel. Supplies were shipped from Drogheda and Dublin to the border city of Carlisle to support English campaigns and men followed the same route. In 1296 Edward I had been impressed by the Irish hobelar, the light horsemen armed with spears. That the Scots should undertake operations in Ireland to discomfort the English is no surprise. What is more, Richard de Burgh, the Red Earl of Ulster and Connacht, had given in marriage to Robert the Bruce his daughter Elizabeth. She was his second wife and bore him four children. This did not discourage Edward Bruce from contemplating displacing de Burgh with the help of certain Irish chiefs with similar interests.

Edward Bruce landed at Larne in the spring of 1315 and was joined by Donal O'Neill of Tirowen and a number of others. Edward was proclaimed King of Ireland and O'Neill later, perhaps in 1317, sent his *Remonstrance of the Irish princes* to Pope John XXII to justify these events, for English kings had been given sovereignty by the pope when Henry II was on the throne. In sum, the document contended that the English had forfeited their rights by failing to honour the terms of their original grant and by subjecting the Irish to oppressive treatment. Edward's forces moved south by the Moyry Pass towards Dundalk which they took and looted on 29 June. Richard de Burgh advanced to oppose them and Donal O'Neill led Bruce away from the superior force at Ardee, south west of Dundalk. They went west of the River Bann through the boggy countryside and across the Blackwater to head north along the western side of Lough Neagh to Coleraine where they destroyed the bridge over the river. Thus, when de Burgh had made his way north by the eastern route, he could not get at them. Meanwhile his forces were draining away. The Connacht men went home and others fell to argument among themselves. The Scots crossed the river on 10 September and the two forces met at Connor, north of Antrim on the north-eastern corner of Lough Neagh. Edward Bruce's victory was decisive, leaving Ulster in his hands with the exception of the castle at Carrickfergus.

There was no alternative to besieging the castle, for Bruce could not contemplate

Lough Neagh, near the mouth of the Blackwater River. The fortified Coney Island provides a refuge. The vast lough, almost an inland sea, and the rivers feeding and draining it shape the military potential of the land as much as the mountains of Ulster.

enlargement of his domains in Ireland with an operational English installation at his back. The fortifications were impossible to storm, so the only course open was to starve out the garrison. Starvation was, at that time, commonplace, for from spring 1315 terrible weather damaged the crops throughout Europe and the suffering continued until 1318. The Keeper of Carrickfergus was Thomas of Thrapston and the proceedings of his trial in Drogheda for alleged treason have been found in the Four Courts in Dublin by G. O. Sayles. From them emerges the fact that, at some stage, a truce was arranged to permit both sides to communicate with one another and one Thomas Dun, a Scot, had been allowed into the castle in pursuit of the discussions and then been permitted to take out two of the prisoners. It had been said Thrapston had offered to join Bruce and that he had sold food to the Scots, but of both these charges he was aquitted. From September 1315 to September 1316 the siege persisted. It is said that thirty Scots who had formed a delegation from Edward Bruce on Midsummer's Day to accept the castle's surrender had been made prisoner. The chronicler Raphael Holinshed says something of their fate in reporting the siege.

> The castell of Cragfergus, after it had been strictly besieged a long time, was surrendered to the Scots, by them that had kept it, till they for want of other vittels were driven to eat leather and eight Scots (as some write) which they had taken prisoners ...

If that is true or not one cannot say. What is clear is that the 'want of ... vittels' imposed the surrender.

Carrickfergus Castle was begun by John de Courcy who built the great, square tower and the southern wall, in the foreground. The northern side was protected by a ditch cut in the rock until, some fifty years later, the great gatehouse and ward were constructed. The castle secures the northern shore of Belfast Lough.

The short reign of Edward Bruce was marked by a series of campaigns through Ireland in which immense damage was done to his adversaries and the innocent alike. The famine that already tormented the land was made worse because Bruce's forces had to live off what they could scavenge and where they took supplies there was nothing left. He set off in November 1315 by Dundalk to Kells where he defeated Roger Mortimer, the Lord of Trim. On he went until he fought again on 26 January 1316 near Ardscull in County Kildare and after that success he continued into Laois and Offaly. He then returned to Ulster. His brother arrived at Carrickfergus in December and in February 1317 the two of them set off once more to make a great sweep south and west, eventually returning in April when Robert went home. The records are then silent on how the next months passed. In October 1318, however, Edward Bruce was moving south again, through the Moyry Pass towards Dundalk. The English moved to oppose him. Holinshed wrote:

> Immediatlie upon his arrival, the lord John Bermingham being generall of the field, and having with him diverse capteins of worthie fame ... led forth the kings power, to the number of one thousand three hundred four and twentie able men against Edward Bruce, who ... was incamped not past two miles from Dundalke with three thousand men, there abaiding the Englishmen, to fight with them if

Dundalk commands the coast road from Dublin to the north. The Norman motte, a short way west of the town at Dún Dealgan, is built on the mound traditionally associated with the legendary Ulster hero Cuchulain. The location was probably the head of the marshy Kilcurry estuary at the time of the Norman advance.

they came forward: which they did with all convenient speed, being as desirous to give battell as the Scots were to receive it.

While the estimate of Bermingham's force may be close to the truth, that of Bruce's has to be treated with caution; it has the ring of a number chosen as the largest that might be believed and impressive enough to suggest the English must have been especially valorous.

Edward Bruce was awaiting his enemies on rising ground at Faughart, just north of Dundalk. He placed his Scots in the front line with the Irish forming a second rank on top of the hill. The Anglo-Irish army attacked with zest, but we have no details of manoeuvre; perhaps there was none, just head-on slogging. Holinshed says:

And herewith buckling togither, at length the Scots fullie and wholie were vanquished, and two thousand of them slain, togither with their capteine Edward bruce. [John] Maupas that pressed into the throng to incounter with Bruce hand to hand, was found in the search dead aloft upon the slaine bodie of Bruce. The victorie thus obteined upon saint Calixtus day, made an end of the Scottish kingdome in Ireland, and lord Bermingham sending the head of Bruce

The graveyard of Old Faughart Church, south of the Moyry Pass, where Edward Bruce lies close to the site of the battle.

The valley of Glenshesk, where Shane O'Neill defeated the MacDonalds in 1564, with Rathlin Island, the O'Donnell stronghold, beyond.

into England, or as Marlburrow hath, being the messenger himself, presented it to king Edward [II] ...

O'Neill's Country

In 1571 an ill-starred and unworthy scheme was put in hand to privatise the colonisation of Ulster. The Enterprise of Ulster, as it is known, was undertaken by two entrepreneurs, Sir Thomas Smith and Walter Devereux, Earl of Essex. Sir Thomas's son, also a Thomas, had only about a hundred men when he landed in the Ards Peninsula, east of Strangford Lough, and was so harassed by Sir Brian MacPhelim O'Neill that they had to spend the winter in Carrickfergus where they endeared themselves to the inhabitants with unruly behaviour. The attempt collapsed in 1573. In August that year Essex's much larger undertaking for the colonisation of County Antrim appeared in Carrickfergus with more than 1,000 men. The Irish united against it, Sorley Boy MacDonnell siding with O'Neill. In 1574 Elizabeth I sent reinforcements and in November that year Essex arranged for the massacre of the Clandeboye O'Neills in Belfast in November. The O'Donnells had acquired Rathlin Island in 1399 and had used it as a refuge in time of crisis ever since. Essex struck in July 1575 and some 600 people – the whole population and the refugees – were killed. The Queen sent Essex her congratulations.

In order to secure the territory further west Essex built defences for the bridge over the Blackwater River near modern Blackwatertown. On the Armagh side an earthen fort was built and a stone tower rose on the north bank. When Hugh O'Neill finally made his opposition to Elizabeth overt in February 1595, this is where he struck, destroying the bridge and the fortifications. Henry Bagenal, marshal of the army and lord of Newry, Mourne and Carlingford, could not be expected to be enthusiastic about this. He was, however, in a difficult position. The policy the government followed was to set up a series of isolated outposts, like the Blackwater forts, and send large bodies of men to their aid if trouble occurred. Armagh was still all right, but Monaghan, to the south west, was now besieged by the MacMahons with Hugh O'Neill's approval. Bagenal had to deal with that problem before the Blackwater crossing could be thought about.

The English forces in Ireland had been reinforced with troops brought back from Brittany, but the experience and organisation of those actually available to Henry Bagenal left a good deal to be desired. In May 1595 he had nineteen companies of foot, both pikemen and men equipped with either muskets or the less sophisticated calivers and known as 'shot', but many of the companies were commanded by mere subalterns. Further there was a lack of officers at a level superior to company commanders which made for poor communications in time of crisis. Bagenal also had six troops of horse, bringing his manpower to the order of 1,750 men. A conversation between one of the captains and the Lord Deputy, Sir William Russell, made it clear that this expedition was seen as a show of strength being made to resupply the garrison at Monaghan rather than as a fighting column, for they were too short of ammunition to act aggressively.

They left Dundalk for Newry and arrived there on 24 May. The next day they headed west for Monaghan via Ballymoyer, near present-day Newtownhamilton. In this area the roads were little more than tracks and movement off them was hazardous because of bogs and rough ground. It remains difficult country today as troops attempting to deal with twentieth-century troubles have found. Sir James Perrot, in the *Chronicle of Ireland*, described it as made of

> ... thick, but especially short and scrubby, woods and thickets, deep and dangerous bogs, steep and craggy hills and mountains, uneven and waterish plashes, straight and narrow passages ...

The English camped at Ballymoyer, near the Owenduff stream, and here they met unexpectedly with Hugh O'Neill. He rode up with his horse to check them out and conducted, as was his wont, a conversation with one of the officers, Sir Edward York, commander of the horse, from the other side of the river. After remarking that the next day would reveal who was master of this countryside, O'Neill withdrew. The next day the English marched on again until they reached the pass at Crossdall, only four miles out of Monaghan. Suddenly they came under attack from a force wearing red coats, English colours.

When Hugh O'Neill had been regarded as an important ally by the English, officers had been sent to train his men and equipment was also provided. No doubt these trained soldiers were now the ones giving lessons to Bagenal's inexperienced infantry. The companies in the vanguard, the front, of the English column had no overall commander and were at something of a loss as to what to do, but Captain Richard Cuney seems to have been chosen or emerged as the commander and he sent a mixed detachment of pike and shot forward to oppose the Irish. Cuney also observed a party of his adversaries making for a wood alongside the road and sent a sergeant out to prevent their taking the place. He got there first and repulsed the Irish. Bagenal sent a message encouraging Cuney to withdraw, but he replied that he 'could better make good that place than come off without more aid' so Bagenal brought up the rest of the column instead and Hugh O'Neill drew off. This was another tactic of which O'Neill was a master, the breaking-off of an engagement at the first sign of uncertainty, only to renew it when it suited him. It was an approach particularly suited to fighting in broken or close country and in time induced as much fear in his enemies as positive attack, the uncertainty proving very unsettling.

The English column completed the journey to Monaghan without further opposition and the stores were delivered. On 27 May at about ten o'clock in the morning the return trip began, heading this time down the Castleblaney road. Bagenal seems to have taken more care with the distribution of officers this time. He took the vanguard under his own command and gave his Sergeant-Major, Sir John Chichester, the control of the 'battle', the main body in the centre of the column. Cuney and one of the captains from the Brittany contingent were in the rear. At Clontibret they intended to turn off to avoid the rising ground to the south and head for Newry, but as they approached they saw Hugh O'Neill's army from afar off. The Earl of Tyrone had

The Gallach Bog at Clontibret, with the land rising beyond it.

received reinforcements, but still his force could not have numbered many more than twice Bagenal's contingent.

The main fight took place just out of Clontibret where the road ran through a bog and under a hill. The English came under fire from the flanks all along the column, but the main weight fell on the unfortunate Cuney's rear-guard. O'Neill had trained his horse and shot, that is his hand-gun men, to work together so that the musketeers covered the cavalry from attack by enemy horse and the horse prevented the muskets being overrun. The objective was to get the sword-wielding cavalry in amongst the opposing pikemen where they could do great damage with less risk and firearms could not be brought to bear on them. The firearms took time to reload and were useless at close quarters except as clubs; the daunting expression 'we fell on with butt-end of musket' occurs often in battle reports from this age. It was the job of the hand-gunners to keep the enemy at a distance as much as to hurt him and both sides expended considerable amounts of ammunition that day to this purpose.

Hugh O'Neill held the pass through which Bagenal intended to go and while the English were halted he hit them as hard as he could. He came very close to being killed himself when one Seagrave saw him beyond the stream and galloped forward with forty troopers to attack him. A version of this incident is possibly included in the writing of Philip O'Sullivan Beare who produced an account of what he thought was the Battle of Clontibret but is, at least in part, the story of Hugh O'Neill's fight with Sir

The road climbs on the left away from the constraint of the bog at the site of the Battle of Clontibret.

John Norris at Mullaghbrack, north of Newry, on 5 September that year. If, for Norris, we read Bagenal, the following may be relevant.

> Norris [Bagenal] being annoyed at his men having been twice repulsed and unable to hold their ground, James Sedgreve [elsewhere called Seagrave], an Irish Meath-man of great size and courage, thus addressed him and Bagnal – 'Send a troop of cavalry with me and I promise you I will drag O'Neill from his saddle.' O'Neill was stationed on the other side of the ford supported by forty horse and a few musketeers surveying the battle thence and giving his orders. For the third time the cavalry and musketeers renewed the fight and Sedgreve accompanied by a troop of picked Irish and English horse charged the ford. In the ford itself a few horse fell under the fire of O'Neill's bodyguard, but Sedgreve rushed upon O'Neill and each splintered his lance on the corslet of the other. Sedgreve immediately seized O'Neill by the neck and threw him from his horse. O'Neill likewise dragged Sedgreve from his horse and both gripped each other in a desperate struggle. O'Neill was thrown under but such was his presence of mind, that prostrate as he was, he slew Sedgreve with a stab of his dagger under the corslet between the thighs and through the bladder.

Other accounts say that one of Hugh O'Neill's men, young O'Cahan, intervened and cut off Seagrave's arm before O'Neill killed his assailant, but O'Sullivan Beare was, one understands, writing to glorify O'Neill. It sounds more impressive if O'Cahan is left out.

Whether this scare led to the English breaking through or not is unclear, but in any case on the English went, fending off further attacks from time to time. Evening drew near and the English, encumbered with wounded, their ammunition running out and tired through and through, still endured the musketry of the Irish who seemed to come and go at will. They eventually halted in growing darkness at Ballymacowen, alongside a bog, or moor as the contemporary reports call it, and rested without abandoning their battle formation. The Irish, no doubt equally exhausted, camped as well. The English set about melting down their Marshall's pewter plate for bullets and sharing out their remaining gunpowder while a servant of Bagenal's, Felim O'Hanlon, made for Newry to seek help. It came as the next day dawned, another 200 men and supplies of ammunition. The Irish drew off to block the Moyry Pass, between Newry and Dundalk, and the shattered English column crept away to shelter in Newry. They had lost 31 killed, and 109 wounded, though this return was certainly doctored to avoid depression. The Irish claimed they had inflicted 700 casualties, so a guess of 300 dead and wounded may not be too far wide of the mark.

The First of the Battles on the Blackwater

The armies of Hugh O'Neill were something new to Ireland. They were far less reliant on foreigners, Scots and the like, hired for fighting by anyone who could afford them, and largely composed of native Irish, bonnachts or billeted men. They were also much better trained and their ranks held soldiers with experience of the continental wars, proficient with their weapons and disciplined, battle-hardened people. Supplies came from Spain in considerable quantities, but also from England in secret and from other European sources according to Hayes-McCoy. He also quotes Lord Deputy Mountjoy:

> ... so far from being naked [i.e. unarmed] people, as before times, were generally better armed than we, knew better the use of their weapons than our men, and even exceeded us in that discipline which was the fittest for the advantage of the natural strength of the country, for that they, being very many, and expert shot, and excelling in footmanship all other nations, did by that means make better use of those strengths, both for offence and defence, than could have been made of any squadrons of pikes or artificial fortifications of towns.

In May 1597 Thomas, Lord Burgh, became Lord Deputy and undertook a new campaign to overcome Hugh O'Neill. Sir Conyers Clifford was to lead a column up the west from Sligo, taking Ballyshannon and pushing up towards Derry on the way to which place Burgh would meet him having advanced by way of Armagh and across the Blackwater. On 12 July Burgh reached Newry with some 3,500 men and pushed on to Armagh. Leaving 1,000 men there he went on at once and got to the Blackwater at two in the morning of 14 July. Hugh O'Neill had built a sconce on the left bank to cover the ford a little downstream of the present Blackwatertown bridge and the alarm was given from there. Burgh's men rushed the ford and took the position, but O'Neill's army prevented any further advance and Sir Conyers's failure to take the O'Donnell castle at Ballyshannon ruined the master plan, so Burgh contented himself with building a new fort on the site of O'Neill's old one. It is doubtful if he ever saw it complete, for he died that October, of typhus. If he did see it he should not have been impressed, for it was a simple thing, a rectangular earthwork with a ditch around it, but lacking flankers that might permit fire along the face of the walls. It was garrisoned with 150 men under Captain Thomas Williams. They had two robinets – light field guns – behind embrasures cut in the parapet and a couple of small fixed guns called *arquebuses-en-croc*.

Just before Burgh died the Irish attacked with scaling ladders but were beaten off. The Irish then undertook a blockade which meant that for just drinking water it was necessary for the English to send out an armed patrol to the river. Food was short and shelter lacking, so by November matters had become serious indeed. However, Hugh O'Neill made truce with the new administration which was to hold for half a year, so the situation eased a little. The English were allowed to cut firewood from specific places and might, if they had had money, have bought food. There were many in government who believed the place should be abandoned and after the end of the truce in June 1598 that decision was very nearly taken. Then Hugh O'Neill resumed antagonistic behaviour and fresh troops arrived in Dublin. This combination of circumstances pushed opinion the other way and Henry Bagenal, the vanquished of Clontibret, was given the task of reinforcing the fort.

Bagenal not only bore O'Neill a grudge because of his mauling of three years before, he also had a personal argument with the Earl. When manoeuvring for power in the face of English ambitions to control the whole of the north, Hugh O'Neill had tried to trap Bagenal into an alliance by eloping with his sister, Mabel. Both professional and family hatred lay between the men.

The English force was a mixed bunch, though numerous at some 4,300 men. There were four companies of veterans from the Picardy campaign (about 500 men) and 900 from the old companies which had served in Ireland for some time past, partly Irish troops but mostly English. The rest of the foot were untrained, undisciplined newcomers. The 300 horse were solid, reliable and experienced. They also had four guns, of which the largest was a saker, a weapon slightly smaller than a six-pounder. This army arrived at camp just north of the ruins of Armagh on Sunday, 13 August 1598. The next morning, on a fine day, they set out to relieve the fort, less than five miles away.

Henry Bagenal knew that Hugh O'Neill's men were ready for them, somewhere between the River Callan which meanders north from Armagh and the Blackwater to the north west; indeed, they had been observed the previous day. He avoided the main highway up the western side of the Callan because the going was better, with only one bog to get over and that would be held against the Irish until branches cut from trees could be laid to allow the wheeled transport to cross. It appears that the route might have passed by way of Cabragh, over the river somewhere near the site of the sewage works close to McCready's Corner and then approximately on the line of the road to Blackwatertown. The column consisted of the six regiments marching some 100 yards apart with cavalry, carts, artillery and so forth between them. Colonel Richard Percy

The landscape south of Blackwatertown, County Armagh. The dense woods have long been felled and the land, in spite of modern drainage, remains boggy. With imagination the scene of the Battle of the Yellow Ford can be recreated in the mind's eye.

commanded one of the two regiments of the vanguard and Bagenal the other. Sir Thomas Wingfield led the main battle and commanded one of its regiments while Captain Cosby headed the other. Colonel Cuney, so much in action on the Monaghan expedition, led the rear-guard and Captain Billings commanded the rear of the regiments. Sir Calisthenes Brooke was General of the Horse. Hayes-McCoy holds that they marched ready for deployment in battle formation, that is, with the pikemen grouped in the centre of each regiment and the musketeers fore and aft, in the way that was to become commonplace in the English Civil War fifty years later. Out in front of the whole force was the forlorn hope, a detached body of skirmishers scouting for contact with the enemy. These were musketeers in two groups, one led by Captain Lee, the other by Captain Turner. On they went, flanked by woods and trees, from which Hugh O'Neill's men subjected them to a continuous peppering of handgun fire.

After crossing the Callan they went over a hill. There are three hills in the narrative, each further along the way to the Blackwater, but it is not possible to locate them with certainty on the ground. Running north east of the principal road between McCready's Corner and Blackwatertown – the B128 on the modern map – are three roads on slightly higher ground, routes on ridges. These three marginally more lofty areas may be the hills the histories speak of. On coming down from the first hill to the valley marked by Bagnel's Bridge Sir Richard Percy's men had to cross a ford which one writer described as a place which oozed discoloured water from the bogs. In the low ground beyond the next hill and before the third Hugh O'Neill's men had dug, across a cornfield, a trench that blocked the way forward and joined up the bogs left and right of the route. They had also plashed, that is cut and woven, shrubbery and small trees in the flanking woods to prevent cavalry having free movement and pits had been dug as traps for the horse as well. Finally, the Irish had marginally more men in the field.

Percy's men got past the ford with its clouded water, the Yellow Ford of the battle's name, and, harrassed from cover as they crossed a clearing, pushed on down through the wooded side of the next hill. They erupted into the cornfield, stormed the trench and thrust on to the top of the third hill. Here they took up a defensive formation to await Henry Bagenal's arrival with the next regiment. In the distance to the north west they could see Captain Williams and his men emerging from the fort with flags flying. At this stage Percy's soldiers felt pretty cheerful and pleased with themselves, although they had lost some men, including Captain Lee of the forlorn hope.

Bagenal was coming on, but a good way behind, and his regiment got a thorough peppering on the second hill. Then came Cosby and far behind him Sir Thomas Wingfield with the saker, their heaviest artillery piece, which kept bogging down, men and oxen heaving together to send it squelching forward before it sank again. At the ford it got severely stuck. To the rear Wingfield could hear gunfire and it was clear that the whole column was getting strung out into its separate parts. He halted his men and rode forward to Bagenal to suggest Percy should be called back and the force consolidated before attempting more, Wingfield himself undertaking to bring up the rearguard to join them. Bagenal sent Percy the order accordingly and then went back with Wingfield to see what was happening. Although the saker had been extracted from the ford, there was still no sight of the rearguard, just the noise of gunfire. Bagenal went forward again to see if Percy had come back. There had been difficulties in obeying Bagenal's orders, as, in Percy's words,

> Our retreat was more in disorder than our going on, because our loose wings, having spent their powder coming in, gave way to the enemy, being both horse and foot, to charge us in the rear, which our new men quitted, and threw away their arms.

Without fire from muskets to cover them, the pikemen were vulnerable to swordsmen. They fell back towards the trench and as they did so the cry came that the Marshal, Henry Bagenal, was dead. The regiment broke. Those who were not killed on one side of the great trench died on the other. Percy himself was knocked down by gunshot which struck his breastplate without penetrating it, but he was rendered semi-conscious and fell in the mud, a circumstance that may have saved his life. He was helped away by his Irish houseboy.

Bagenal had been coming on with his regiment towards the trench and to Percy's aid when, raising the visor of his helmet to see what was going on, he was hit by a musketball and killed at once. The few remains of Percy's men joined Bagenal's, now commanded by Captain Evans, who were engaged in assaulting the trench. Wingfield was now in overall command, and he decided they had to pull back to Armagh. Then yet more problems beset them. The saker's carriage broke and the gun was irretrievable. Finally, a musketeer replenishing his powder flask allowed a spark from his glowing match to fall into the gunpowder barrel. It, and a second barrel next to it, blew up in spectacular fashion, the report goes. Quite who survived as an eyewitness to the musketeer's folly is unclear, but that the two barrels exploded is incontestable. By this time the rearguard had crossed the ford, so the better part of five regiments, in order of march Bagenal's (now Evans's), Cosby's, Wingfield's, Cuney's and Billings's, were between the ford and the top of the second hill.

When the decision to retreat had been made Cuney went to sort out his rear-guard regiments and Wingfield went forward to give Cosby his instructions. By the time he reached him Evans's and the fragments of Percy's had been driven back up the second hill from the cornfield, and although clearly ordered to guard the rear of the retreating army, Cosby joined Evans in advancing to the relief of the desperate men. More than that, they passed Percy who was trying to gather up his survivors, and pushed on towards the fatal trench. The move was a failure. Their men could take no more and broke. Evans died and Cosby was captured. Wingfield got news of Cosby's disobedience and its consequences, so he took a squadron of horse and managed to extract about 500 men from the fight and bring them back to join Cuney. Wingfield then took charge of a new rear-guard. Billings, meanwhile, had thwarted an attempt by Hugh O'Neill to seize the ford at their rear and the battered force was able to make its way back to Armagh. There they made what fortification they could amongst the ruins to pass the night.

The cost was high. Twenty-five officers and more than 800 men had been killed, and another 400 had been wounded. About 300 deserted to Hugh O'Neill. The Irish lost 200 dead and 600 wounded, it is estimated. The fort was surrendered, but O'Neill did not follow up the victory by attacking the defeated army in Armagh. His reasons for sparing it are not known, but Wingfield was permitted to lead it away to Newry and thence, by the Moyry Pass, out of Ulster.

The Moyry Pass

Entry to and exit from Ulster on the east is by the Moyry Pass, a deceptively mild and open-looking place, but one which confines the commander of a large body of men to a limited and vulnerable route through hills and between bogs that favour irregular forces as much today as in the past. It was natural for Hugh O'Neill to exploit the place. He had dealt with Robert Devereux, Earl of Essex, whom Queen Elizabeth had sent in April 1599, by prevarication and cumbersome negotiation. The men had met at a river ford somewhere between Drogheda and Drumcondra where

> Tirone and all his company, stood up allmost to theire horsses bellies in water, the L. Lieutenant with his, upon harde grounde. And there Tirone spake a good while, bare headed, and saluted with a greate deale of respect all those which came downe with the L. Lieutenant. After almost half an howres conference, it

The railway, centre left, heads north from the Moyry Pass, near the castle. The countryside, south Armagh, has been debatable territory from early times.

Moyry Castle was built by Lord Mountjoy in an attempt to secure the Gap of the North after Hugh O'Neill's eventual withdrawal from the position.

was concluded there should be a meeting of certayne commissioners the next morning ...

The beguiling of his enemies into endless negotiations was a technique in which Hugh O'Neill excelled and which many have adopted since. Elizabeth was unimpressed with Essex's performance.

> We never doubted but that Tyrone whensoever he sawe anie force approache, ether himselfe or anie of his principall partisans, wold instantly offer a parley ...

Charles Blount, Lord Mountjoy, replaced Essex the following year. He gave Sir Henry Docwra free rein in the north west and it was when distracting Hugh O'Neill from Docwra's landing at Derry that he first experienced the difficulties that the Moyry Pass could impose. He had gone back to help the convoy that was being brought up behind him by the Earl of Southampton and Captain Blayney and found them blocked by O'Neill. When they saw Mountjoy coming down behind them, the Irish promptly shot around to the other side of the convoy and attacked there in a hand-to-hand encounter occasioned by the heavy rain which wet everyone's powder. That was a mere skirmish.

On 20 September 1600 Mountjoy was on the move north again and camped at Faughart, on the hill on which Edward Bruce fought his last battle. He had about 3,000 foot and 300 horse. A scouting party went forward and as they did so Hugh O'Neill withdrew before them. That night they harassed wood-gatherers and fired shots at the English camp. Then they tried seducing the English horse into an ambush, but before any more substantial action could begin it started to rain. It rained heavily and steadily for four days. On 25 September there was only mist to cause a difficulty and Captain Thomas Williams, the survivor of Blackwater Fort, led a reconnaissance in strength down into the pass. The way narrowed and the hills rose beside them, covered with bushes and trees. They came on some Irish sentinels whom they brushed aside and then found a trench across the path which was abandoned as they approached. Another trench a little further on was taken and then the Irish resistance solidified. They fought their way back out of the pass to bring the intelligence to Mountjoy, having lost seven dead and thirty wounded, but claiming to have given the Irish more than a hundred casualties.

The trenches were no trivial ditches, but solid great barricades. Mountjoy's secretary, Fynes Moryson, is reported by Hayes-McCoy as saying the Irish

> raised from mountain to mountain, from wood to wood and from bog to bog long traverses with huge and high flankers of great stones, mingled with turf and staked on both sides with palisadoes wattled.

There were three such structures south of the stream called Three Mile Water, a tributary of the river draining towards Dundalk. Moyry Castle, which was built the following year to secure the place, overlooks the stream along the old road to the north east, and the third and last of these trenches was across that road south east of the

Crannógs, artificial islands, were constructed in loughs for refuge and defence. This example is at Lough na Cranagh, east of Ballycastle, County Antim.

castle. Beyond Three Mile Water was another stream, Four Mile Water, where the convoy of the previous year had been held up. And beyond that who knows what further devices Hugh O'Neill had contrived? The weather continued wet and it was not until 2 October that they saw action. The Irish came riding down in force and the English responded to the challenge. There was a hotly fought series of skirmishes as the Irish drew their enemies deeper into the pass, but by the time, about three hours later, they were at the third entrenchment it was clear to Mountjoy that they could not break through. They then had to fight their way out again. On 5 October they tried again, but this time Sir Charles Percy took about 230 men high to the west, along the hillside, to enfilade the Irish fortifications. Sir Oliver St John was sent in support. The Irish saw them coming and formed a conventional line of about 300 soldiers to meet them. The Irish advanced firmly and the fight was closely balanced until musketeers from St John came clambering up to shoot at the Ulstermen and put them to flight. By that time the English were spent both here and in the pass below; the attack failed.

The English at Faughart church were cold, wet and miserable. Many were sick, as were many of their horses. Mountjoy made another outing on 6 October, but then withdrew. Within a week Sir Samuel Bagenal was on his way north to Newry, but by the coast road through Carlingford and along the side of the lough. On 13 October Hugh O'Neill vacated the pass entirely and pulled back to his island stronghold, a crannóg in Lough Lurcan, between Newry and Armagh. His reasons are not clear. It is possible he foresaw himself being surrounded in the pass if forces at Newry were sufficiently reinforced and men came up from Dundalk, or possibly he was over-extended and had to pull back closer to the heartland of his strength, or, finally, it could have been another throw in his game of alternate fight and talk. In any case, the English who took over the pass were mightily impressed with his works and relieved they had not been called upon again to force a way through. Mountjoy was to find his satisfaction at Kinsale in the following year.

Back to the Blackwater

In the confused time of the English Civil War, on 23 October 1641, the opportunity was taken by Sir Phelim O'Neill, Conor Maguire and Hugh Óg MacMahon, to raise an insurrection with a proclamation. It included the statement,

> [We] are inviolably resolved to infix ourselves in an immutable and pure allegiance for ever to his Royal Majesty and his successors. Now it is that the Parliament of England, maligning and envying any graces received from his majesty by our nation and knowing none so desired of us that of religion, and likwise perceiving his Majesty to be inclined to give us the liberty of the same ...

The reaction of the Puritan government in England was predictable, but it was their agreement with the Scottish Parliament that eventually brought an army into Ulster to put down the rebellion against Parliament. In June 1642 Owen Roe (Eoghan Ruadh) O'Neill returned from the Low Countries, where he had been in the Spanish service against the Dutch and then the French with his own regiment, and denounced the excesses of the Celtic Ulstermen whose deeds fuelled the myth of Catholics massacring Protestants. In that year also Parliament sent English forces to Ireland and the Scots sent 10,000 men under General Robert Monroe. He took Carrickfergus and based himself there before adding Newry to the territory he dominated. On 9 January 1642 the Scots were responsible for the slaughter of some 3,000 Irish Catholics at Island Magee, and explained their policy of wholesale massacre of men, women and children with the observation, 'Nits make Lice.' It is curious that the Scots and Monroe are not held in the same loathing as Cromwell and his countrymen, but perhaps there is not the same political payoff to be had.

Owen Roe O'Neill found the Irish in Ulster ill-equipped, poorly organised and insubstantial. They did hold the Fort of Charlemont on the Blackwater north of Armagh and further downstream than the fortification involved in the Yellow Ford fight. It was a square, demi-bastioned earthwork built in 1602 with a house within and an outer bawn or enclosure as well, reaching towards the bridge over the river; the earthworks of the modified layout survive. In the next couple of years after Owen Roe O'Neill's arrival there were small confrontations and skirmishes, but he for the greater part used the country of Cavan, Westmeath and Longford as a refuge rather than as a base for aggression. In 1645 the arrival of the Papal Nuncio and Archbishop of Fermoy, John Baptist Rinuccini, with money and weapons transformed the situation. By the spring of 1646 Owen Roe O'Neill had assembled an army of some 5,000 men, seven regiments of foot and seven troops of horse at the Hill of Gallanagh near Lough

In June 1602, during Mountjoy's operations against Hugh O'Neill, a campaign fort was built at Charlemont, near the mouth of the Blackwater. By 1624 it had been developed into a rectangular, bastioned fort of which the entrance gate still stands.

Sheelin, east of Granard in Longford. They were stiffened with his own men from his continental campaigns and given firm training.

In 1646 Monroe had planned to link with two other forces, one led by his son-in-law, Colonel George Monroe, coming from Coleraine on the northern coast, and the other by Sir Robert Stewart marching from the Foyle valley and Derry. Monroe himself, coming from Carrickfergus, was at Poyntz Pass, north of Newry, on 4 June and Stewart at Clogher, west of Armagh. They were all to meet at Glaslough, a little to the west of Armagh. Owen Roe O'Neill responded by leaving the Hill of Gallanagh at the end of May. He had intelligence from Charlemont and other sources and knew what his enemies were doing. He reached Glaslough on 3 June and moved on to Benburb, on the Blackwater upstream of the old fort, in the middle of his converging adversaries. They had to fight him and his position was to his advantage, the river limiting his enemies and Charlemont available for refuge.

One of Monroe's officers on his way to meet the Coleraine force on 4 June captured an O'Neill soldier in Armagh and sent him back to Monroe for questioning. The news that Owen Roe O'Neill, with 6,000 men, was marching to Benburb galvanised the Scotsman into action. His army of 6,000 men and 600 horse hurried forward, but was too late to catch the Irish on the march. Indeed, the whole thing may have been a

Benburb Castle stands high above the Blackwater.

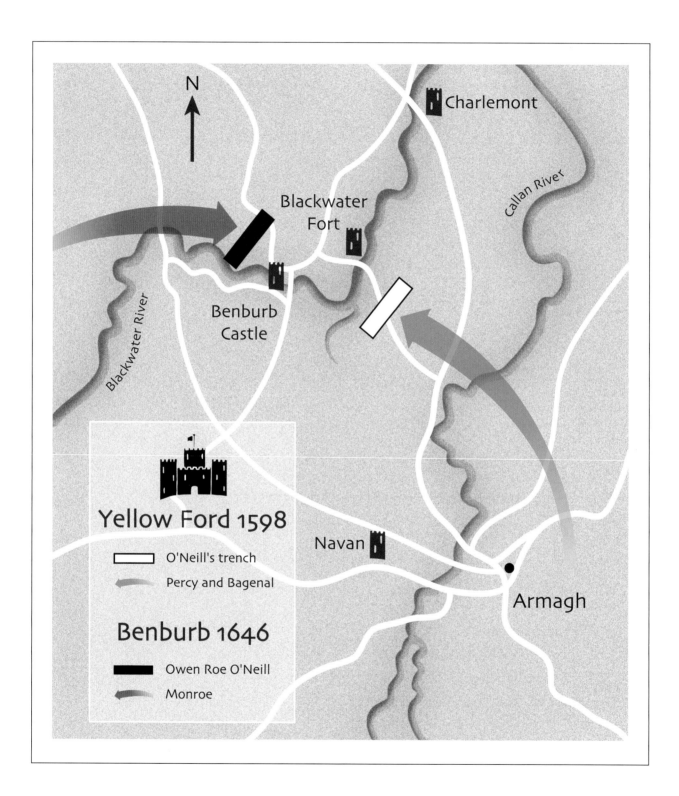

plant, for the captured man almost certainly came from the camp already established at Benburb. Be that as it may, Monroe's blood was up. On Friday 5 June he arose early and went to see for himself. He found O'Neill next to the old castle and the two peered at each other across the river. Monroe obviously could not cross here, nor downstream where he could be caught between the Benburb and the Charlemont men. He would have to cross at Caledon, upstream, if he was to get at his enemy and stop him escaping. Moreover, his son-in-law was marching south from Coleraine and Owen Roe O'Neill would be caught between the two of them. By three o'clock in the afternoon Monroe's army had crossed at Kinard on their way to Caledon and then they pushed north for Benburb. Meanwhile O'Neill sent Lieutenant-Colonel Brian Roe O'Neill, most of the cavalry and a small group of foot to head for Dungannon to hold up Colonel George Monroe.

Robert Monroe's route took him over the River Oona north west of the modern Battleford Bridge, but before that he had to deal with a delaying tactic set up by Owen Roe O'Neill. The Irishman had sent out a force of some 1,000 men west of the Oona to occupy the wooded Knocknacloy Hill overlooking the road at Tullygiven Lough and the adjacent bog. In this action, known as Ballaghkillgevill, the bog may not have been an impressive obstacle. The bog a mile or so away at Drumflugh was described at that time by Massari, Rinuccini's assistant, as being dried out entirely by the hot weather. Lieutenant-Colonel Cuningham of Glencaim's Regiment led the advance with 500 men and a brisk exchange of fire took place at six o'clock. The advance guard was thrown back but the commander of the horse, Viscount Montgomery of Ards, brought his cavalry up and the Irish retired through the brush where the horse could not follow. Owen Roe O'Neill had used the time gained to draw up on the hill at Drumflugh, just west of Benburb and he also entertained, one imagines, hopes of the men sent to deal with Colonel Monroe returning to help here. His men were in battalions, that is blocks of pikemen perhaps eight rows deep with musketeers on each flank. There were four battalions in the front line and three, covering the gaps in the front line, made up the second line.

Monroe's army deployed itself on the hill of Derrycreevy, where the Red House now stands, with a little tributary of the Blackwater across his front. They were in two lines with the Blackwater on his right and the aforementioned, dried-out, bog on his left. His cannon were in front. The position was too narrow for his manpower and the chance of his cavalry being able to come from the rear between his battalions was small, but there was no choice. Monroe's cannon opened up and his cavalry took Owen Roe O'Neill's force on its left flank to drive it away from the river. O'Neill's remaining horse charged bravely and pushed the Scots back. It seems the Scots-English soldiers were now very tired, for they had made marches of more than fifteen miles two days in succession. Both sides stood exchanging fire for a while and then horsemen appeared from the north. Both sides hoped they were theirs. They were Brian Roe O'Neill's men from whom, thinking they were being attacked by the whole of Owen Roe's force, the Coleraine column had run. It was about eight o'clock. Owen Roe O'Neill gave the order for a general attack, crying, 'Give not fire till you are within Pike length!'

The line of the stream across the field of the Battle of Benburb is marked by trees. Monroe's army occupied the hill to the left.

The northern coast at White Park Bay, Co. Antrim.

The Irish wave rolled forward, pikes presented, and the two armies locked in battle. They came, as the expression was, to 'push of pike' and that phrase conjures up a true and terrible picture. Once their weapons had been discharged the musketeers had no time to reload before their enemies were on them, so they reversed their guns and used them as clubs, they 'fell on with butt end of musket'. It was a brutal, bloody business. Monroe's horse attempted to break up the attacking ranks but, as a contemporary observer said, 'fell pell mell amongst our foot'. The effort to consolidate the Scots by drawing the front line back into the second was fruitless because the lack of room led to confusion in the ranks. Monroe's left was smashed and the whole line rotated until they had their backs to the river and the setting sun in their eyes. And so they died, perhaps as many as three or four thousand of them. Irish losses were trivial. Owen Roe O'Neill had proved himself master of the set-piece battle. He had, however, the misfortune to be allied with lesser men.

The Rising of 1798

The rising in Wexford and the invasion of the French get most of the attention, but the attempt to overthrow the British government was never a religious movement and, given the participation of the anti-clerical French, could be seen as the very opposite. The American and French examples were of liberty and government growing from the people and as acceptable in Protestant areas as elsewhere, but the United Irishmen was a fragmented movement and the risings in the various regions of Ireland were uncoordinated and thus vulnerable to suppression. In Ulster the plan was to rise in Down and Antrim, astride Belfast, and action commenced at the end of May. On 6 June the Presbyterian-born Henry Joy McCracken wrote a proclamation setting the rebellion in motion and by the next morning the commander of the northern garrison, Major-General George Nugent, having an efficient spy system, knew all about it.

The first objectives of the rising were the strategically important towns of Antrim, north west of Belfast on the shore of Lough Neagh, and Ballynahinch, south of Belfast. The former commanded the route from Belfast to Derry and the latter was in the centre of County Down. Domination of these towns was to lead to territorial gains that would pinch out Belfast and include the fall of government garrisons guarding the access routes by sea at Carrickfergus on Belfast Lough, and by land from the south along the coach road from Dublin, Lisburn, Hillsborough and Banbridge. To secure Antrim McCracken needed to hold Toom, and thus the bridge over the River Bann as it left Lough Neagh, Randalstown, between Toom and Antrim, Crumlin to the south and Templepatrick on the road from Belfast. He led his men to Donegore Hill, high above Antrim, and there assembled about 3,000 men. Randalstown had been taken swiftly by a force under Samuel Orr and that then split into three, part going on to Toom, part remaining to hold the place and the greater section setting off to join their comrades at Antrim. A rising at Larne on the coast to the north east eventually secured the town and more men set off for Antrim. By the night of 7 June much of the county was in United hands.

The town of Antrim was not heavily defended. Lord Massereene had about fifty yeoman infantry, seventy dragoons and a couple of dozen civilian volunteers. He elected to hold the market house and the castle. McCracken led his force from the east into the town in the early afternoon and sent a party to take the church while the larger part of his force went down the main street. As he did so 150 men of the 22nd Light Dragoons, sent by Nugent, hurried into the town from the south. The plan to block that road had failed, and, indeed, McCracken seems to have taken no precautions at all to cover his rear. The dragoons made the classic error of charging pikemen and recoiled. As they did so Orr's men were marching into town from the west and, seeing dragoons approaching and unaware they were in retreat, the newcomers took fright and fled.

More government men were coming up and Colonel Clavering brought two five-inch howitzers which he set up outside town and started lobbing shells in. The desperation and fear that must have gripped the English is clear from such an idiotic action. Soon another 400 or more yeomanry and dragoons had flooded into Antrim, shooting virtually at random, killing rebels and loyalists alike. Probably 300 died for a cost of about 60 killed and wounded on the government side. However, much of the rest of the county was still up in arms. General Nugent took the prudent course of offering an amnesty if people surrendered their weapons. It worked and the rising in Antrim simply deflated.

As peace broke out in the north east, war began to the south. On 9 June the United Irishmen took Saintfield and Newtownards, south and east of Belfast. Under the command of a man of Scottish Protestant lineage, Henry Monroe of Lisburn, they concentrated at Saintfield, a force of about 7,000 men. An English Colonel, one Stapleton, attempted to attack them and was lucky to get away with his life and relatively little damage to his small troop. The triumphant rebels moved towards Ballynahinch where the Ards division occupied Montalto, the country estate of Lord Moira, and the army camped on Ednavady Hill.

General Nugent came from the north while another government force approached from Downpatrick, the south east. Comber, halfway between Saintfield and Newtownards, had been garrisoned with about a hundred men to prevent a flight into the Ards Peninsula. Nugent had 1,500 men and artillery, six six-pounders and two howitzers. As they advanced they put Saintfield to the torch and then found an outpost of rebels on Windmill Hill on the Saintfield side of Ballynahinch. Colonel Stewart's Scotch Fencibles drove them off and hanged one unfortunate from the windmill. Nugent then subjected the town to shellfire until ten that night.

The rebel force began to crack, and during the night the deserters numbered in the hundreds. In the morning skirmishing broke out in the town as looters from the government side met pikemen from the United ranks and it seemed the rebels might get the upper hand, but Stewart took his Fencibles and two cannon to attack the Montalto camp and smashed away with grapeshot. The pikemen attempted to attack, but were blown away by the gunfire.

The *London Gazette* carried a letter from Dublin, dated 14 June.

> ... intelligence arrived this day from Major-gen. Nugent, stating, that on the 11th inst., he had marched against a large body of rebels who were posted at Saintfield. They retired on his approach to a strong position on the Saintfield side of Ballynahinch, and there made a show of resistance, and endeavoured to turn his left flank; but Lieut-col. Stewart, arriving from Down with a pretty considerable force of Infantry, cavalry, and yeomanry, they soon desisted, and retired to a very strong position behind Ballynahinch. Gen. Nugent attacked them the next morning at three o'clock, having occupied two hills on the left and right of the town, to prevent the rebels from having any other choice than the mountains in their rear for their retreat. He sent Lieut.-col. Stewart to post himself with a part of the Argyle fencibles and some yeomanry, as well as a detachment of the 22nd light dragoons, in a situation from which he could enfilade the rebel line, which Col. Leslie, with part of the Monaghan militia, some cavalry, and yeoman infantry, should make an attack on their front. Having two howitzers and six six-pounders with the two detachments, the Major-general was enabled to annoy them very much from different parts of his position. The rebels attacked impetuously Col. Leslie's detachment, and even jumped into the road from the Earl of Moira's demesne, to endeavour to take one of the guns; but they were repulsed with slaughter. Lieut.-col. Stewart's detachment was attacked by them with the same activity, but he repulsed them also; and the fire from his howitzer and six-pounder soon obliged them to fly in all directions ... About 400 rebels were killed in the attack and retreat ...

By seven o'clock in the morning Monroe's men could take no more and a general flight began, with the usual loss of life. Part of Ballynahinch was burnt down and the rebellion in Down also came to an end. The *London Gazette* had another letter from Dublin dated 19 June.

> ... since the defeat of the rebels at Ballynahinch, advices have been received from Major-Gen. Nugent, that they have not reassembled in the county of Down, but are submitting and delivering up their arms in various places.

In a letter three days earlier the report had been that rebels were petitioning for pardon and offering to give up their arms. Nugent had promised to accept on condition that they gave up Monroe to him and all the other 'principal traitors who had instigated them to their late wicked practices ...' Monroe was caught on the morning of 15 June. Both he and McCracken were hanged, but instead of the wholesale murder and pillage that took place elsewhere, this phase of the rising of 1798 ended on a quieter and more humane note. A purely political uprising, 1798 was the last occasion on which political ends would be pursued without the addition of religious difference.

Sources

General

A number of books have provided the foundation for this work, chief amongst them being Hayes-McCoy's *Irish Battles*. Next in importance have been *A Military History of Ireland* and *A History of the Irish Soldier*. In seeking a context for events rather more broadly drawn I have used *The Oxford Illustrated History of Ireland* and *The Oxford Companion to Irish History*. Of particular value have been those works that quote extensively and verbatim from contemporary writings, notably David Willis McCullogh's *Wars of the Irish Kings* and Tom Reilly's *Cromwell*. In considering terrain, the Ordnance Survey of Ireland's Discovery Series, 1:50,000 mapping, has been very useful. Works consulted in addition to these are included in the list below.

Ashley, Mike, *British Monarchs*, London: Robinson Publishing, 1998.

Bartlett, Thomas, and Keith Jeffery, eds., *A Military History of Ireland*, Cambridge: Cambridge University Press, 1996.

Bray, William, ed., *Memoirs of John Evelyn, Esq., F.R.S.*, London: Frederick Warne, no date.

Bredin, A.E.C., *A History of the Irish Soldier*, Belfast: Century Books, 1987.

Connolly, S.J., ed., *The Oxford Companion to Irish History*, Oxford, Oxford University Press, 1998.

Duffy, Seán, ed., *Atlas of Irish History*, Dublin: Gill & Macmillan, 2000.

Foster, R.F., ed., *The Oxford Illustrated History of Ireland*, Oxford: Oxford University Press, 1989.

Gravett, Christopher, *Norman Knight*, London: Osprey Publishing, 1993.

Harrison, Mark, *Viking Warrior*, London: Osprey Publishing, 1993.

Hayes-McCoy, G.A., *Irish Battles: A Military History of Ireland*, Belfast: Appletree Press, 1989.

Lee, J. J., *Ireland 1912-1985*, Cambridge: Cambridge University Press, 1989.

McCullogh, David Willis, *Wars of the Irish Kings*, New York: Three Rivers Press, 2002.

Marix Evans, Martin, *The Military Heritage of Britain and Ireland*, London: André Deutsch, 1998.

Roche, Richard, *The Norman Invasion of Ireland*, Tralee: Anvil Books, 1970.

Sweetman, David, *The Medieval Castles of Ireland*, Cork: The Collins Press, 1999.

Tierney, Mark, *Ireland since 1870*, Dublin: C.J. Fallon, 1988.

Dublin and the Pale

The Cromwell campaign is a delicate subject in Irish history, as are the events of the Anglo-Irish War and the Irish Civil War. I have depended on the books listed below on these and other topics. Florence O'Donoghue's account of Easter Week 1916 from Hayes-McCoy's *The Irish at War* has, among others, contributed to my description of events.

Gardiner, S.R., *History of the Commonwealth and Protectorate*, Vol. I, London: Longmans Green, 1903.

Hayes-McCoy, G.A., ed., *The Irish at War*, Cork: The Mercier Press, 1964.

Hopkinson, Michael, *Green Against Green: The Irish Civil War*, Dublin: Gill & Macmillan, 1988.

Kinross, John, *The Boyne and Aughrim*, Moreton-in-Marsh: Windrush Press, 1997.

Reilly, Tom, *Cromwell: An Honourable Enemy*, Dingle: Brandon, 1999.

The Achilles Heel of the South East

In addition to subjects relying on sources mentioned above, particularly Tom Reilly, this section deals with the '98 Rising, another tough subject and another minefield for a writer attempting objectivity. I have used extracts from the *London Gazette* as reprinted in *The Gentleman's Magazine* because they are contemporary and the bias is so evident that it scarcely needs comment. I have also drawn on Thomas Pakenham's *The Year of Liberty* and Bartlett, Dawson and Keogh's book on the 1798 rebellion. Charles Dickson's account of the Battle of New Ross, in Hayes-McCoy's *Irish*

Battles, underpins my narrative of that fight. In connection with the Military Road, Paul Kerrigan's book on Irish castles and forts has its first, but not its last, use for this work.

Bartlett, Thomas, Kevin Dawson and Dáire Keogh, *Rebellion, A Television History of 1798*, Dublin: Gill & Macmillan, 1998.

Grose, Francis, *Military Antiquities Respecting a History of the English Army*, Vol. II, London: Stockdale, 1812.

Kerrigan, Paul M., *Castles and Fortifications in Ireland*, Cork: Collins Press, 1995.

Pakenham, Thomas, *The Year of Liberty*, London: Hodder & Stoughton, 1969.

Urban, Sylvanus, ed., *The Gentleman's Magazine and Historical Chronicle for the Year MDCCXCVIII*, London: St John's Gate, 1798.

The Narrow Doors of Munster

For detailed information on the history of Bantry Bay I have made selective use of Michael Carroll's *A Bay of Destiny*. John Thuillier's *History of Kinsale* has augmented the standard works most helpfully. For the difficult topics of the War of Independence and the Civil War I have drawn on, without necessarily accepting wholesale, Charles Townshend, Tom Barry and Richard Bennett, and Michael Hopkinson's *Green Against Green* which I also used in the first chapter. I have also made some use of Peter Hart's *The IRA & Its Enemies*, but this book is not the place for an in-depth study. Interested readers are warmly encouraged to explore Hart's work for themselves. Paul Kerrigan (see above) and Andrew Saunders are the source of information on fortifications.

Barry, Tom, *Guerilla Days in Ireland*, Dublin: Anvil Books, 1962.

Bennett, Richard, *The Black and Tans*, Staplehurst: Spellmount, 2001.

Carroll, Michael J., *A Bay of Destiny: A History of Bantry and Bantry Bay*, Bantry: Bantry Design Studios (Publications), 1996.

Hart, Peter, *The IRA & Its Enemies: Violence and Community in Cork 1916-1923*, Oxford: Oxford University Press, 1998.

Saunders, Andrew, *Fortress Britain: Artillery Fortification in the British Isles and Ireland*, Liphook: Beaufort, 1989.

Thuillier, John, *History of Kinsale*, Kinsale: 2001.

Townshend, Charles, *The British Campaign in Ireland 1919-1921*, Oxford: Oxford University Press, 1975.

The Western Flank

In respect of both Dysert O'Dea and Knockdoe the accounts from McCullogh's *Wars of the Irish Kings* have added light and shade as, in the case of Aughrim, have the contemporary quotes included in John Kinross's *The Boyne and Aughrim*. Kerrigan is the single source for fortifications in the region and Townshend once again provides the basis for the twentieth century conflict.

Delany, Ruth, ed., *The Shell Guide to the River Shannon*, Dublin: ERA-Maptec, 1996.

Joyce, Martin J., *The Battle of Aughrim*, Aughrim: no date.

The Far North West

The inclusion of the only mythical battle, and it may well be a perfectly real one in some ways, was prompted by the availablity of Elizabeth A. Gray's translation of *The Second Battle of Mag Tured* in McCullogh's *Wars of the Irish Kings*. The military history and fortification titles mentioned above have supplied much of the rest of the information. The work of the Chevalier de Latocnaye comes from Sean McMahon's anthology. In respect of the 1798 invasion and risings I have used Bartlett, Dawson and Keogh as above and drawn heavily on Pakenham's *The Year of Liberty*. The passages from the *London Gazette* are quoted from the *Gentleman's Magazine* of 1798.

Anon., *Forthill Park*, Enniskillen: Fermanagh District Council, no date.

Kennedy, Conan, *Ancient Ireland: The User's Guide*, Killala: Morrigan Books, 1997.

McMahon, Sean, *The Derry Anthology*, Belfast: The Blackstaff Press, 2002.

The Mountains of Ulster

The part of the *Book of Howth* which underpins the account of Norman activity was found in McCullough's *Wars of the Irish Kings* as was some of the material that contributed to the story of Edward Bruce. The papers of Sir John Harrington, which recount the doings of the Earl of Essex, are from that source also. In addition to Hayes-McCoy's *Irish Battles*, articles by Clive Hollick in *Battlefield* threw light on the Battle of Benburb. Pakenham and Bartlett, Dawson and Keogh were, again, the foundation for the United Irishman rising story.

Hollick, Clive, 'The Battle of Ballaghkillevill, 1646', *Battlefield*, January 1994.

Hollick, Clive, 'The Campaign and Battle of Benburb, 1646', *Battlefield*, July 1993.

Index